The Final Piece

The Final Piece

A Systems Approach to School Leadership

Lee A. Westberry

ROWMAN & LITTLEFIELD
Lanham • Boulder • New York • London

Published by Rowman & Littlefield
An imprint of The Rowman & Littlefield Publishing Group, Inc.
4501 Forbes Boulevard, Suite 200, Lanham, Maryland 20706
www.rowman.com

6 Tinworth Street, London SE11 5AL, United Kingdom

Copyright © 2021 by Lee A. Westberry

All rights reserved. No part of this book may be reproduced in any form or by any electronic or mechanical means, including information storage and retrieval systems, without written permission from the publisher, except by a reviewer who may quote passages in a review.

British Library Cataloguing in Publication Information Available

Library of Congress Cataloging-in-Publication Data

ISBN 978-1-4758-5873-0 (cloth)
ISBN 978-1-4758-5874-7 (pbk.)
ISBN 978-1-4758-5875-4 (electronic)

Contents

Acknowledgments	ix
Introduction	xi
STUDENT SUPPORT SYSTEMS	**1**
1 Guidance Systems	3
Guidance Counselor Role	4
Guidance Data Points to Consider	5
Small Groups	8
At-Risk Populations	10
Graduation Plans	12
Systems Approach	14
Progress Monitoring	15
Summary	17
A Piece-at-a-Time	17
References	18
2 Multitiered Systems of Support	21
Definition	21
Looks can be Deceiving	22
Tiers of Intervention	23
Leadership	25
Processes	25
Step One	27
Step Two	27
Step Three	27
Step Four	28
Step Five	29

	Step Six	30
	Catch 'em if You can	31
	Progress Monitoring	32
	Summary	32
	A Piece-at-a-Time	33
	References	33
3	Mentoring Programs	35
	School-Based Programs	36
	Business and Industry Mentors	40
	Alliances	41
	Systems Perspective	42
	Data Collections	43
	Surveys	46
	Summary	49
	A Piece-at-a-Time	50
	References	50
4	Outside Agencies	53
	Needs Assessment	53
	School-based Needs Assessment	54
	Community-based Needs Assessment	55
	Resources in Your Community	57
	State Agencies	57
	Local Agencies	58
	Neighborhood Agencies in Charleston, SC	58
	Relationships	58
	A Systems Approach	60
	Summary	61
	A Piece-at-a-Time	62
	References	62

THE CULTURE SYSTEM   **63**

5	School Culture System	65
	Growth Mindset	65
	Principal Role	66
	District Role	67
	Community Role	69
	Feedback	70
	Moving Parts	71
	Evaluation	72
	Systems Approach	73

	Summary	75
	A Piece-at-a-Time	75
	References	76
6	Support	77
	School Community	77
	Parents and Students	77
	Booster Clubs	82
	Civic Organizations	83
	District Community	84
	Business Support	85
	Business Partners	85
	Academy Partners	87
	Cheerleading	91
	Systems Perspective	92
	Progress Monitoring	92
	Summary	93
	A Piece-at-a-Time	94
	References	94
7	School and Community Communications	97
	Communication within a School	97
	Announcements	97
	Emails	98
	Call-out Systems	100
	Halls and Walls	102
	Meetings	103
	Community Communications	105
	Marquee	105
	Newsletters	106
	News Media Outlets	107
	Churches or Social Gathering Places	109
	Social Media	110
	Web Pages	112
	Systems Approach	113
	Summary	113
	A Piece-at-a-Time	116
	References	117
Conclusion		119
About the Author		121

Acknowledgments

I would like to acknowledge my oldest daughter, Warner Westberry, who created the cover art for this book. She has a servant leader's heart and aspires to serve others through art therapy.

I would also like to acknowledge my colleagues at The Citadel Zucker Family School of Education for their unwavering support in my endeavors.

Introduction

In *Putting the Pieces Together: A Systems Approach to School Leadership*, the focus was on the first two systems needed in effective school leadership: curriculum and instruction and teacher support systems. In this volume, *The Final Piece: A Systems Approach to School Leadership*, the focus will be on the last two systems to complete the construction of our schoolhouse. Remember the analogy used in the first book of constructing a schoolhouse, wherein the systems perspective provided the foundation. This is the lens that is needed in all school leadership endeavors.

The next step in the systems building process included the vertical framing, or outer walls, which provided the form and function of our house—the system of curriculum and instruction, for teaching and learning is the purpose of educational institutions. Therefore, that system must come first. Principals need to understand their roles in this vital system and how to operate within. See figure 0.1 to refresh your memory.

The second system discussed in the first book included the additional vertical supports, and they represent the teacher support systems. Curriculum and instruction provide the teacher with direction and purpose; however, teachers require more supports in order to maximize effectiveness. Instructional leaders must develop a system in which administrative and teacher roles work together for the benefit of students.

Remember, the answers to juggling the principal responsibilities lie in the systems approach used in the four major systems. This book will focus on the final two systems: student support and culture systems. These four systems must operate simultaneously for maximum effect. Neglecting one system any time can cause damage and minimize the effectiveness of the other systems.

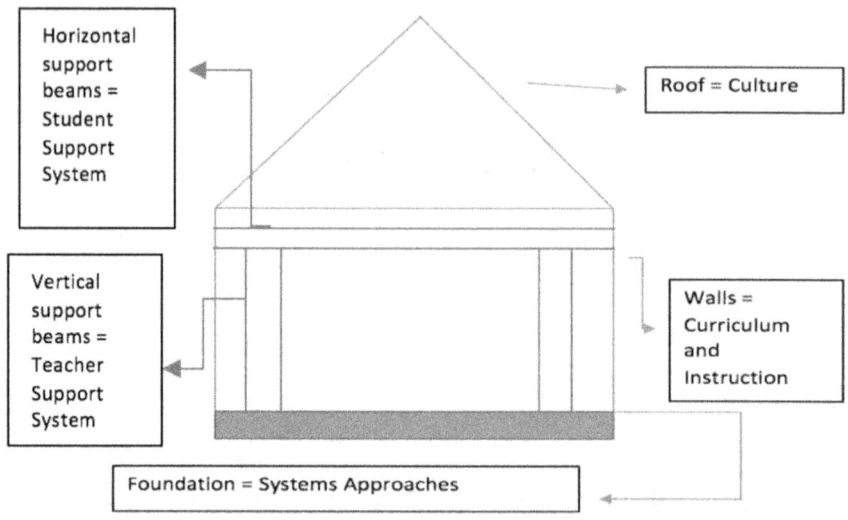

Figure 0.1 Systems Approaches.

STUDENT SUPPORT SYSTEMS

In building the schoolhouse, the foundation (systems perspective), the exterior walls (curriculum and instructional system), and the vertical supports (teacher support system) have been established. The next step is to erect the horizontal support beams, or the student support system. Imagine the logic in this construction for a minute. The exterior walls include the major system of teaching and learning, and these walls form the shape of the house (the purpose). The teacher support system, or vertical supports, helps to hold up the student support systems.

Administrators need to fully develop student support systems in order to "catch kids" before they fall. Too many students, today, do not have the proper guidance at home. Often, this lack of guidance is from lack of understanding or identification of the real issues students face. Schools have to be concerned with more than just teaching and learning to because today's students face more problems than many can imagine. Student support systems, therefore, must be multifaceted and include guidance, multitiered systems of support, mentoring, and the use of outside agencies.

Chapter 1

Guidance Systems

Do more than belong: participate. Do more than care: help. Do more than believe: practice. Do more than be fair: be kind. Do more than forgive: forget. Do more than dream: work.

—William Arthur Ward

To provide guidance, by definition, is to provide direction. Students need direction as they navigate their way through school systems, family issues, personal issues, peer issues, community issues, and future planning. To tell the truth, students today have more issues to deal with growing up than past generations. Just watch the nightly news if you question that statement.

Additionally, parents may not be as well-equipped to deal with many of the issues facing students today because they themselves did not have to deal with the pressures and dangers of social media; the abundance of knowledge available to students through the internet, whether appropriate or not; changing governmental legislation like marijuana laws; and escalating community violence in the face of the country's politics, and so on.

The guidance office is a hub of activity and is often separate from administrative offices; as such, are administrators really in tune with the demands and pressures of the guidance office? Too often, guidance is overlooked as a point of valuable data for educational leadership. Guidance departments can maintain an understanding of the true needs of the school and community.

GUIDANCE COUNSELOR ROLE

The guidance counselor role often shifts when considering grade-level configurations. For example, elementary counselors are often tapped to teach exploratory guidance classes with students. Middle-school counselors may do the same, but they also conduct transition meetings for students exiting to the high school as well as deal with the myriad of student concerns, such as bullying. High-school counselors are inundated with graduation plans, or career counseling, for all students grades 9–12, registrations, testing (in some areas), course scheduling, and so on.

Of course, not all districts and schools support counselors being involved in all of these areas, such as scheduling, but the truth is that high-school counselors are consumed with many job duties besides counseling at times. All grade band counselors find less and less time to spend with students conducting actual counseling because of the myriad of demands that are placed upon counselors. Just as administrators, the counselor's role has morphed to include more responsibilities.

To understand the complexity of counseling at the multiple grade-level configurations, one must understand the developmental needs of each grade configuration. Elementary students are beginning to develop their self-concept about academics, personal values, decision-making skills, and attitudes about school, peers, and social groups (Solomon, 2013). This pivotal time in a student's life will set the stage for how students engage in school and peer groups for years to come. Elementary school counseling programs should provide a healthy foundation for supporting this developmental period, and a program, good or bad, will have a lasting impact on students (Setiawan & Ismaniati, 2019).

Middle-school students are trying to find where they fit in the world. They struggle with their self-identity as the peer group becomes more influential. Middle schoolers want to assert themselves as more mature learners and individuals, but they truthfully still need the guidance provided to elementary students because they are more sensitive to the perceptions of others. These students are growing rapidly and are becoming more aware of social issues; as such, personal identification, prevention, and intervention programs become more important in the lives of these students (Kuperminc, Leadbeater & Blatt, 2001).

High school is the final transition into the world of adulthood. What does that look like for students? Work? Postsecondary education? High-school students will explore and define their independence as they embark on the journey of life, but the peer influence is great because with that independence and freedom of movement, these students face more risky behaviors within those peer groups. Every decision made can impact what comes after high school, and these students need a support system to help them navigate academic and peer pressures, as well as deal with the next steps, such as college applications, financial assistance, and career exploration.

GUIDANCE DATA POINTS TO CONSIDER

The counseling model as described by the American School Counselor Association (ASCA) addresses the demands of school counselors and goes further to outline the types of services that should be provided. ASCA describes counseling services in three categories: direct student services, indirect student services, and program management and school support services (ASCA, 2012). See table 10.1 for a description of each type of service.

Moreover, ASCA suggests that 80 percent of a counselor's time be spent in direct and indirect services with only 20 percent of time spent in program management and school support services (ASCA, 2012). With the ever-present issues of mental health in our society, one really cannot argue logically with that time configuration. However, this time allotment is difficult for many school counselors to abide by.

Think about those counselors who are directed to create the school's master schedule, coordinate school testing, or participate in lunch duty. Do either of these school activities fit in the categories above? The answer is no, but these duties are often ascribed to counselors. A typical sample counselor week of time and activities should look like table 1.1, according to the ASCA model (ASCA, 2012).

The only way for administrators to support the appropriate time considerations for guidance counselors and for counselors to advocate for their departments is for counselors to track their time each day. A simple Excel spreadsheet would suffice if designed appropriately. This tracking of time will provide valuable data for administrators on the needs of the school as well. Data on time spent with student counseling, small group counseling, and even paperwork will help guide the strategic plan for guidance programs. See figure 10.3 for a simple time analysis tracking system that will allow for concrete time to be calculated and help ensure time is being spent where it is intended.

From the time tracker, counselors can obviously determine data points for the following: the number and type of crisis counseling sessions, the number and type of individual counseling sessions, the number and type of small group sessions operating and when they are meeting, and so on.

This data is important for counseling departments and also for administrators. The data will inform principals and districts of the needs of the students and will inform curriculum development and professional development needs of counselors and teachers.

Table 1.1 ASCA Model Description of Services (ASCA, 2012)

Direct Student Services	Indirect Student Services	Program Management and School Support Services
Assist students to set personal goals	Referrals to outside agencies	Advisory councils
Assist students to develop future plans	Consultation and collaboration with teachers to support students	Annual agreements
Small group counseling	Consultation and collaboration with administrators to support students	Action planning with counselors and administrators
Individual counseling to meet immediate student concerns/needs	Consultation and collaboration with community partners	Data analysis/Needs assessment
Counseling curriculum for academic, social, and career development		Student records

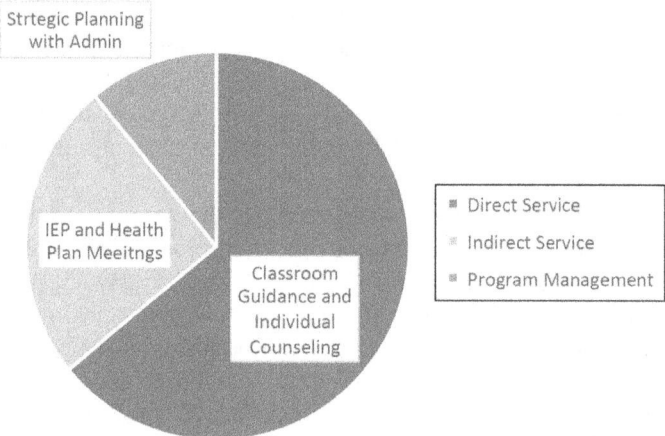

Figure 1.1 Ideal Typical Counselor Week of Time/Activities Sample Counselor Week of Time/Activities Aligned with ASCA (2012).

For example, if a large number of threat assessments for harm to self are being conducted at a school, the school staff may need professional development on recognizing signs of depression in teens. If a number of threat assessments are being conducted for harm to others, the local law enforcement may need to intervene as well. Categorizing and recognizing patterns of behavior within the building will help inform administrators of necessary steps in order to provide a safe and secure environment conducive to learning.

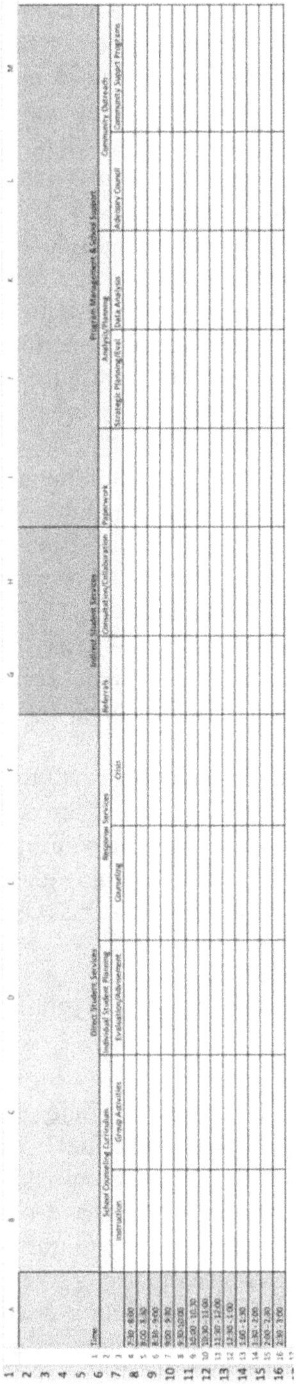

Figure 1.2 Guidance Time Analysis.

Other data points to consider include referrals to outside agencies or collaboration with staff. The sheer absence of these interventions tells an administrator that counselors are not included in intervention planning, as they should be. Counselors can share information about children as much as teachers sharing information with counselors. Likely, at least one adult knows the background of a student that may inform interventions needed. Counselors should be a part of this conversation.

Time spent with performing duties outside of the ASCA model also informs the administration that counselors are being pulled too much from their assigned duties. This will allow administration to restructure duties and responsibilities so that counselors are able to perform their jobs to the best of their ability. No one wants to hear the excuse that a child was not receiving the proper support because counselors were too busy with master scheduling or testing, for example, to assist a child.

Administrators should work with a counseling department to set goals and track the progress of those goals. Identifying the needs should be the basis of any goal-setting activity. Therefore, the data from the tracker will help identify some needs in the school, as they should become a focus of service delivery. Part of the program management and school support activity involves surveys of students and parents to find out what they think. Annual surveys may be given on the frequency of risk-taking behaviors in high school, for example. Surveys on incidences and feelings of bullying in middle schools would also be appropriate.

Students and parents need to have input into the guidance programs in a school, and surveys provide a way to focus the programs on where the services are needed. These are additional data points that must be considered. A focus on mental health and decision-making with social skills should play a role and be considered (Carney, Kim, Hazler & Guo, 2017).

SMALL GROUPS

Small group counseling is an effective way for counselors to address the needs of students with similar issues in a safe, inclusive, and manageable environment (Gerrity & DeLucia-Waack, 2007; Paisley & Milsom, 2007). The benefit of small group counseling sessions is that trust can be built more quickly in a more intimate setting: students have to trust the adults before any real work can begin, just like teachers have to trust administrators before any real change can occur within a school.

Additionally, students in small counseling groups can identify with the other students in the group who have similar issues or concerns, eliminating the feeling of isolation which can be detrimental. In this environment, students can learn from one another on how to cope with issues. This type of counseling also affords students the opportunity to belong—a basic need of humans (Maslow, 1970; Tucker et al., 2019).

Small groups, in schools, are designed to improve academic and social behaviors as well as change perceptions of acceptable behaviors. Parental perception of student needs should be consulted, as stated above, via surveys and conferencing. Teachers can also provide insight into academic behaviors and attitudes that may help design small group counseling sessions. Unfortunately, guidance small group counseling can be one of the guidance components that is underutilized. Often, time constraints in the upper-grade configurations limit group counseling, possibly when that method of counseling is needed most.

Obstacles to counselor time, as mentioned earlier, may include counselors being pulled to perform duties outside of the recommended model. However, there are other obstacles to counselor time effectiveness, and one obstacle may be the assigned caseload of counselors. If counselors are assigned so many students that they cannot effectively deliver all services needed, small group counseling may be the first program to be cut.

ASCA recommends that each counselor be assigned no more than 250 students per counselor (ASCA, 2012), but school budgets do not always allow this caseload. For example, in the 2016 school year, the average caseload in the United States was well above the recommendation, topping 450 students per counselor (Gewertz, 2018).

Another obstacle to group counseling includes accountability. Teachers are so concerned about the loss of instructional time due to accountability measures, and rightfully so, that support to pull students from classes to administer group counseling is not always prevalent. Ideally, students could meet after school, but attendance would be poor due to motivation and transportation. A solution is to pull students from exploratory and elective courses, but this is the time that students should be exploring career interests and enjoying the arts without the intense academic pressures of the core curriculum.

Group counseling can be tracked via the aforementioned tracker, and results can be monitored and evaluated easily. If a small group is designed to meet monthly and help academically struggling students focus on time management and study skills, the results can be shown in student achievement results. The same can be said for groups designed for school apathy and poor attendance; attendance rates and achievement can be monitored for the students who belong to the group.

What about small groups designed to help students make better choices, such as teen pregnancy groups? Students are faced with so many pressures today both from home and from peers that groups based on making smarter choices allow students to speak honestly about those pressures. Certainly, these groups should focus on risk-taking behaviors as well as connecting these students with community resources that may help to break a cycle of poor choices.

AT-RISK POPULATIONS

Today, schools are more intensely focused on at-risk populations with new accountability measures, such as graduation rates. What determines that a student is at risk, and more importantly, how can guidance programs help? Students can be determined to be at risk if they are intellectually capable but do not perform at expected levels, are intellectually challenged and become frustrated, or have a low motivation to achieve. Symptoms of at-risk students become apparent in poor grades, attendance, and behaviors. As students progress through the grades, the symptoms hold true.

In a study by Chen and Kaufman (1997), they found that students are considered at risk if they possess one or more of the following characteristics: low socioeconomic status from a single-parent family, a family member dropped out, the students experienced frequent changes in schools, the student had average grades of "C" or lower in middle school, and/or the student repeated a grade. Students were tracked through high school from middle school, and the dropouts were found to possess at least one of the characteristics described.

In a study of elementary students, Rush and Vitale (2010) identified eight characteristics, in that they identify students as at risk for becoming high-school dropouts as they progress through the fifth grade: academically behind, behavior and poor coping skills, social withdrawal, family income, poor parenting, language development, grade retention, and poor attendance. In essence, the basic identifiers exist for students who are at risk, and those identifiers remain consistent. So, what can guidance programs do to help these students?

At-risk students need first to be identified in schools (Cook et al., 2014; Fryer, 2017). Monitoring student records is a good place to start. Knowing which students are overage for their grade, have attendance issues, suffer poor academic grades, and experience more behavior problems should be a topic of consideration. Counselors and administrators, together, should discuss these students to decide what interventions are needed. Planning ahead for these students may help them experience some success and serve as a motivation rather than merely administratively responding to their failures.

Of course, small group sessions, mentioned above, are a good tactic to use with some students. Students and school officials need to understand that students do not have the luxury of selecting some of these indicators for themselves: family history, socioeconomic status of families, and parental circumstances. However, students do have the luxury of selecting their futures with hard work and assistance. Sometimes, students do not understand the control they do have in their lives, and guidance counselors can help them to see the light.

Additional individual counseling can be very beneficial for these students. In one South Carolina high school, counselors were each assigned a caseload of at-risk students. Counselors met with their students one-on-one every two weeks to check in on student progress, help set up tutoring sessions, and discuss any concerns students had. The relationships built with those counselors tremendously helped those students feel a sense of community as well as know that the school served as a support.

Academic achievement, behavior, and discipline were tracked for these students. Success was noted when students earned their credits and moved on to the next grade level. The rate of recidivism for students appearing on the at-risk list was lower than expected. Students who did not progress as hoped were referred to another school program for support. The point is that the counselor connection made a difference in most cases. See figure 1.3 for a sample counselor tracking system.

Sometimes these at-risk students need help connecting to community resources that will help their families. It is unquestionably hard for students to focus on school and academics when their families are fighting to survive. Guidance programs can serve as key support for struggling and misplaced families. More on community resources will come later. Note that high-school dropouts are at a higher risk of substance abuse; therefore, interventions are critical beyond educational aims (Reingle Gonzales et al., 2016). Guidance counselors can serve as the bridge to help families with preventative measures.

Lastly, teachers need to fully understand at-risk students, and counselors and administrators can help in this endeavor. Most teachers have not experienced the conditions in which many at-risk students live. Honestly, many teachers will have no frame of reference to understand their at-risk students. Therefore, it is crucial to educate them. Not only will professional development help support effective strategic planning for these students, but counselors need to be part of the conversations when teachers discuss their struggling students.

Counselors can help teachers understand why a student may not consistently have his homework or why he may appear sleepy and disengaged in class. Without that understanding, teachers can become frustrated with what they consider apathetic or disruptive students without understanding the children themselves. This understanding leads to better accommodations, student

	A	B	C	D	E	F	G	H	I	J	K	L	M	N	O
				1st Progress											
1	Counselor Interventions	Grade	At Risk Factors		IC	GC	PC	LH	CS	ST	TC	AT	RA	RO	
2	Individual Counseling (IC)														
3	Group Counseling (GC)														
4	Parent Conference (PC)														
5	Letter Home (LH)														
6	Coping Skills (CS)														
7	Study Time (ST)														
8	Teacher Conference (TC)														
9	Assigned Tutoring (AT)														
10	Referral To Administration (RA)														
11	Referral To Outside Agency (RO)														
12															
13	NAME														
14	Doe, John	9	Failing 1 or more course	Eng = 57, Alg 1 = 59	x						x				
15	Doj, Kim	9	Failing 1 or more course	Bio = 42	x						x				
16	Elton, Job	10	Attendance	9 absences	x	x	x				x		x		
17	Frank, Frank	11	Failng US History, 7 referrals	US Hist = 52, 3 ISS, 2 OSS	x		x	x							
18															
19															

Figure 1.3 Sample Counselor Tracking System.

engagement, empathy, and support. With the proper support, at-risk students can become quite successful (Clark, Cobb, Finn & Rock, 1997; Dynarski et al., 2008).

GRADUATION PLANS

High-school students are faced with making big decisions about their futures, and one of those decisions is whether to go to college, go to work, or go in the military after graduation. Counselors play a pivotal role in helping students make those decisions; however, the counseling program must include the parents in the discussion. Parents are the largest influence on career aspirations of high-school students (Smith, 1991). Therefore, counselors must help educate the parents on career choices based on student academic attainment, skills, and interests.

Graduation planning is not a one-time event, either. Conversations need to be held multiple times over a student's school career, starting in elementary school. Elementary counselors help students to understand what careers are available to them as they help students explore their interests. Of course, all counselors need to stay abreast of the changing workforce and the jobs that may exist. Elementary children most often relate to what they know: doctor, lawyer, policeman, teacher, fireman, and so on. However, so much more exists in today's changing society.

Middle-school counselors should continue with the same exploration and interest identification while advising students on courses to take in high school, as well as the grades and education needed for the career paths chosen

(Mau, 1995). Continued exploration in branches of a profession needs to ensue (Mobley et al., 2017). For example, so many more areas exist in the medical field other than the traditional roles of doctor/nurse. Middle-school students can understand the opportunities that exist outside of the traditional roles. Parents need to be part of these conversations as well so that they understand their children's strengths and opportunities that exist for them.

Let's face it; career opportunities have changed radically with the addition of technology. Jobs that exist today did not exist twenty or even ten years ago. What about the jobs that will exist in five years? Therefore, parents need the education along with their students, as parents need to carry on the conversations at home. Students need to always have a focus on their learning with goals to achieve. Otherwise, students may find that their chosen career path is not possible due to poor choices and insufficient preparation, and that is a tragedy.

Counselors need to also understand the cultural differences among groups and educational aspirations and expectations (Mau, Hitchcock & Calvert, 1998). One shoe does not fit all, so varied programs for the different career paths are pivotal to family support. Success is not defined in the same manner by all students and families, and that is ok. However, most parents want their children to be successful, which is defined. Therefore, schools and counselors must provide programs that understand that most families have the same values, but they may experience different beliefs on how to attain that success.

So, graduation planning should be a focus of conversation starting in elementary school. Goal-setting serves as a motivation for achievement in all facets of life (Button, Mathieu & Zajac, 1995; Dubrin, 2012) and schools are no different. Elementary teachers often ask students what they want to be when they grow up. This is the first stage of goal-setting and graduation planning for these students. With counselor education in elementary schools and middle schools, these goals should be reviewed and adjusted based on interests, abilities, and course requests each year.

Once students enter high school, these goals should be expanded to include strategies of attainment with timelines attached. For example, financial aid applications and deadlines need to be adhered to and supported through student and parent programs. Additionally, college applications with early admission decisions are due by December of the student's senior year for most colleges and universities. Therefore, Scholastic Aptitude Test (SAT) scores or American College Testing (ACT) scores need to be available to submit by December itself.

So, students need to start taking these tests in their junior year in high school and not wait until their senior year, in case they need to take it again in order to attain a desired score. If a student wants to enter the military, then times need to be set to take the military entrance exam and preparation needs to begin much earlier. Sophomore students need to plan for what happens in their junior year as far as testing, college explorations, internship, and apprenticeship opportunities go. In essence, all four years of high school should be spent planning.

This type of planning will help students and families understand the process of post high school planning and what resources are available. For example, do colleges offer free application times, and if so, when? What about testing waivers for free testing for those who qualify? Parents and students need to be informed early on in their high-school careers so that proper planning and preparation can take place. Guidance programs should be strategically planned with parents to help support the transition of students beyond high school, but the focus should always be on what comes after high school.

If schools are merely focused on students graduating from high school, student aspirations may not extend beyond that point. However, if the conversation is always about the next steps beyond high school, students and parents become conditioned to expect the next step. As B.F. Skinner (1938) noted in his theory of operant conditioning, a person will make an association between a behavior and a consequence if it is repeated. In this case, counselors are continuously reinforcing decision-making and behaviors with success beyond high school.

Not only was Skinner on track but so was Robert Merton with his Self-Fulfilling Prophecy Theory. According to Merton (1948), in essence, a behavior will become true if it is believed to be true; if schools believe that students will be successful beyond high school, then students themselves will believe they will be successful beyond high school. School counseling programs need to understand their power and influence among the students they serve; furthermore, counseling programs need to capitalize on this influence early on.

SYSTEMS APPROACH

In order to plan for guidance systems, administrators should use the ASCA model in planning programs strategically. The needs assessment, based on student, parent, and teacher feedback as well as school data, should inform that strategic plan. Imagine the plan is organic and changes are based on the student and community needs. See figure 1.4 for an example of a beginning plan for counseling programs.

In the below example, school data may show that the at-risk population is academically not performing well and on-time graduation rates among this subgroup has a 38 percent gap between their counterparts. Therefore, small groups and individual counseling may be necessary to positively impact this

Guidance Systems 15

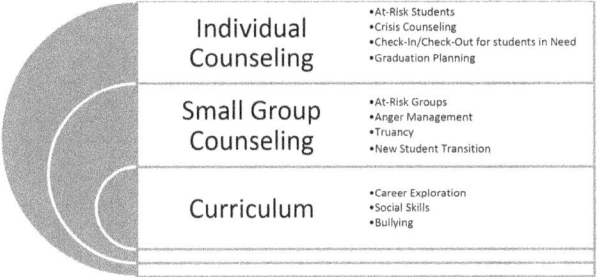

Figure 1.4   Example of Counselor Planning.

group. Additionally, the number of special needs students requiring a check-in/check-out system requires that guidance counselors are utilized as well as administration personnel. This type of program planning serves as an intervention before a problem arises.

Furthermore, graduation planning is critical; so, those graduation plan meetings are for all students in the school and will consume a big portion of counselor time. Consequently, administrators must work with counselors to block the time needed to conduct these meetings while allowing counselors to be available for crisis counseling, individual and group counseling sessions. Time management and scheduling are critical to the success of all programs.

When planning the guidance programs, administrators must take into consideration the staff and caseloads as well as resources and other personnel. Administrators themselves may be called upon to assist with groups or crisis counseling, and that is to be expected. Therefore, planning takes on a whole new element. Administrators must also follow through with data collection for each element of the plan to determine if the programs are working or what needs to be changed. See figure 1.5 for a sample of a full counseling strategic plan.

PROGRESS MONITORING

By mapping out the programs and program evaluations that should exist, administrators can collect data throughout the school year to determine effectiveness. Without having a plan, the programs may be hit or miss, and children cannot afford a miss. Just as administrators should have data meetings with their teachers, administrators should have data meetings with their counseling departments once a month. These data meetings should include the time analysis trackers as well as the program evaluations and effectiveness.

Counselors are often left to their departments and provide a once-a-year report to their advisory council and administration, but reporting at the end

Counselor Strategic Plan

	Individual Counseling				Group Counseling					Curriculum				
Program	Timeline	Personnel	Evaluation	Program	Timeline	Personnel	Evaluation	Curriculum	Timeline	Personnel	Resources	Evaluation
At-Risk Students	Every 2 weeks	25 students/counselor	Grades	At Risk Groups	Once a Month	Guidance Counselor	Survey	Career Exploration	1x/month	Guidance Counselor	$1,500	Student Survey
			Attendance				Attendance			Home Room Teacher		
			Credits Earned				Discipline	Social Skills	1x/month	Guidance Counselor	$500	Discipline
			Discipline Reports				Grades					Guidance Referrals
			Course requests	Anger Management	Once a Month	Guidance Counselor	Discipline Reports	Bullying	4x/year	Home Room Teacher	$1,500	Guidance Referrals
Graduation Planning	Twice a year @ year	Every Counselor	Parent feedback			Mental Health Counselor	Teacher Reports					Discipline
		Alphabet distinctions by counselor	College Applications				$500					Student Survey
			Scholarship Applications	Truancy	Every 2 weeks	Guidance Counselor	Attendance					
			Work Study	New Student	Every 2 weeks for first month then once a Month	Guidance Counselor	Teacher Reports					
			Apprenticeships				$1,000					
			Military Enlistments									
Check-In/Check-Out	Daily	Counselors assigned by IEP Teams	Grades									
		Administrators assigned by IEP Teams	Discipline Reports									
			Attendance									
Crisis Counseling	As Needed	Guidance Counselor	Rates of Recidivism									
		Mental Health Counselor	Grades									
		School Psychologist	Discipline Reports									
			Attendance									

Figure 1.5 Sample Counselor Strategic Plan.

of a year does not allow for adaptations when needed to maximize effectiveness. Therefore, counselors should expect that school accountability is shared within their departments as well so that changes can be made real time to best serve the students.

Furthermore, school counselors must know they have the full support of the administrative team and therefore should discuss resources needed and obstacles faced while trying to implement the planned program. Administrators and counselors should work together to remove the obstacles to the best of their ability. Progress monitoring of guidance programs is a way to offer better support to guidance programs while ensuring programs are having the impact intended—serving the children.

SUMMARY

Guidance programs are an integral part of any school, and administrators need to understand that guidance programs are a large part of student support systems. Guidance programs that follow the ASCA National Model for School Counseling Programs delineate time allocations to 80 percent of time spent on direct and indirect services to students. The other 20 percent allocation of time is spent on program management and school support.

Direct and indirect student services include individual counseling, crisis counseling, group counseling, and curriculum development. Guidance departments should track their time to ensure quality guidance programs. Administrators need to understand limitations of time and not delineate too many job responsibilities outside of the scope of work for counselors. Only by adhering to the purpose and function of guidance programs can students be served effectively.

Guidance programs should be planned based on a needs assessment that includes school data, student input, parental input, and teacher input. Once program needs are identified, they should be strategically planned to include an evaluation component. Counselors should be a part of the accountability system and report data for each program to determine effectiveness. Administrators, through the course of data conversations with guidance departments, will better understand the needs of the department and of the school community.

A PIECE-AT-A-TIME

- How do guidance counselor roles shift with grade-level configurations?
- How are guidance program needs determined? Based on what?

- What national model should be used when considering guidance programs?
- What are the time allocations in this model and how are they calculated?
- What are the three different types of direct services to students?
- What are the three different types of indirect services to students?
- What is the importance of graduation planning?
- What are the types of group counseling that would be effective in your school?
- How do you identify the types of group counseling needed?
- What are the indicators of at-risk students?
- How do administrators progress monitor guidance student support programs?

REFERENCES

American School Counselor Association (2012). *ASCA National Model: A framework for School Counseling Programs* (3rd edition). Alexandria, VA: Author.

Button, S., Mathieu, J. & Zajac, D. (1995). Goal orientation in organizational behavior research. *Organizational Behavior and Human Decision Processes, 67*, 26–48.

Carney, J. V., Kim, H., Hazler, R. J. & Guo, X. (2017). Protective factors for mental health concerns in Urban middle school students: the moderating effect of school connectedness. *Professional School Counseling, 21*(1). doi: 10.1177/2156759X18780952

Chen, X. & Kaufman, P. (1997). Risk and resilience: The effects of dropping out of school. Paper presented at the *American Association of Educational Research (AERA)*, Chicago, IL.

Cook, J. & Kaffenberger, C. (2003). Solution shop: A solution focused counseling and study skills program for middle schools. *Professional School Counseling, 7*, 116–123.

Cook, P. J., Dodge, K., Farkas, G., Fryer, R. J., Guryan, J., Ludwig, J., . . . Steinberg, L. (2014). The (surprising) efficacy of academic and behavioral intervention with disadvantaged youth: Results from a randomized experiment in Chicago (NBER Working Paper No. 19862). Retrieved from http://www.nber.org/papers/w19862

DuBrin, A. J. (2012). *Essentials of management*. Mason, OH: Cengage South-Western.

Dynarski, M., Clarke, L., Cobb, B., Finn, J., Rumberger, R. & Smink, J. (2008). *Dropout Prevention: IEC Practice Guide*. National Center for Education Evaluation and Regional Assistance. US Department of Education: NCEE 2008-4025.

Finn, J. D. & Rock, D. A. (1997). Academic success among students at risk for school failure. *Journal of Applied Psychology, 82*(2), 221–234.

Fryer, R. G. (2017). The production of human capital in developed countries: Evidence from 196 randomized field experiments. in: Duflo, E. and Banerjee, A. (Eds.), *Handbook of Field Experiments* (pp. 95–322). Amsterdam: North Holland.

Gerrity, D. A. & DeLucia-Waack, J. L. (2007). Effectiveness of groups in the schools. *The Journal for Specialists in Group Work, 32*, 97–106.

Gewertz, C. (2018). School counseling: State-by-state student-to-counselor ratio report: 10-year trends. *Education Week, 14*, 5.

Kuperminc, G., Leadbeater, B. & Blatt, S. (2001). School social climate and individual differences in vulnerability to psychopathy among middle school students. *Journal of School Psychology, 39*(2), 141–159.

Maslow, A. H. (1970). *Motivation and Personality* (2nd edition). New York: Harper and Row.

Mau, W. C. (1995). Educational planning and academic achievement of middle school students: A racial and cultural comparison. *Journal of Counseling and Development, 73*, 518–526.

Mau, W. C., Hitchcock, R. & Calvert, C. (1998). High school students' career plans: The influence of others' expectations. *Professional School Counseling, 2*(2), 161.

Merton, R. K. (1948). The self-fulfilling prophecy. *The Antioch Review, 8*(2), 193–210.

Mobley, C., Sharp, J., Hammond, C., Withington, C. & Stipanovic, N. (2017). The influence of career focused education on student career planning and development: A comparison of CTE and non-CTE students. *Career and Technical Education Research, 42*(1), 57–75.

Paisley, P. O. & Milsom, A. (2007). Group work as an essential contribution to transforming school counseling. *The Journal for Specialists in Group Work, 32*, 9–17.

Reingle Gonzalez, J., Salas-Wright, C., McConnell, N., Jetelina, K., Clipper, S. & Businelle, M. (2016). The long-term effects of school dropout and GED attainment on substance abuse Disorders. *Drug and Alcohol Dependence, 158*(1), 60–66.

Rush, S. & Vitale, P. (1994). Analysis for determining factors that place elementary students at risk. *The Journal of Educational Research, 87*(6), 325–333.

Setiawan, A. & Ismaniati, C. (2019). The effectiveness of cooperative learning approach with students teams-achievement division and numbered head together to improve elementary school students' social skills. Conference proceedings of the *3rd International Conference on Current Issues in Education (ICCIE'18)*.

Skinner, B. F. (1938). *The Behavior of organisms: An Experimental Analysis*. New York: Appleton-Century.

Smith, T. (1991). Agreement of adolescent educational expectations with perceived maternal and paternal educational goals. *Youth and Society, 23*, 155–174.

Solomon, G. (2013). Fair play in the gymnasium: improving social skills among elementary school students. *Journal of Physical Education, Recreation, and Dance, 68*(5), 22–25.

Tucker, J. R., Wade, N. G., Abraham, W. T., Bitman-Heinrichs, R. L., Cornish, M. A. & Post, B. C. (2019). Modeling cohesion change in group counseling: The role of client characteristics, group variables, and leader behaviors. *Journal of Counseling Psychology*. Advance online publication. doi: 10.1037/cou0000403

Chapter 2

Multitiered Systems of Support

Be strong, be fearless, be beautiful. And believe that anything is possible when you have the right people there to support you.

—Misty Copeland

Student support comes in many forms and is delivered through multiple avenues. The last chapter discussed guidance systems of support, with a focus on social/emotional aspects and career counseling; however, a schoolwide system of academic support is needed. Guidance cannot do the work of student support alone. Most states employ a framework of support aimed at helping all students learn what is called a Multitiered System of Support (MTSS). This framework should serve as a guide to understand the multiple supports needed to help students learn and grow.

DEFINITION

What is MTSS? According to the Center on Response to Intervention at American Institutes for Research (2014), MTSS is defined as the following:

> Multi-tiered system of support (MTSS) is a prevention framework that organizes building-level resources to address each individual student's academic and/or behavioral needs within intervention tiers that vary in intensity. MTSS allows for the early identification of learning and behavioral challenges and timely intervention for students who are at risk for poor learning outcomes. It also may be called a multi-level prevention system. The increasingly intense tiers (e.g., Tier 1, Tier 2, Tier 3), sometimes referred to as levels of prevention

(i.e., primary, secondary, intensive prevention levels), represent a continuum of supports. Response to intervention (RTI) and Positive Behavioral Interventions and Supports (PBIS) are examples of MTSS. (p. 6)

In order to provide a continuum of support, systems need to be identified in advance so that students can move through the levels of support without interruption.

Teachers need to understand the levels of intervention and what resources are readily available to them in helping students succeed. Otherwise, time lapses and teacher frustration only serve to delay and prohibit support. When teachers get frustrated, students experience negative effects (Assor, 2005; Liu, Bartholomew & Chung, 2017; Wlodkowski, 1978).

LOOKS CAN BE DECEIVING

Administrators must remember that academic struggles can manifest themselves in different ways: poor attendance, behavioral issues, and poor performance. These red flags are evident in schools; however, these behaviors are often attributed to causes besides academic struggles. Teachers and parents, for that matter, can become frustrated with behaviors that appear to be laziness or disinterest.

Unfortunately, students can become labeled for displaying symptoms of the real cause of the problem, academic deficiencies, and this can affect teacher interactions with students (Bartusch & Matsueda, 1996; Damico & Augustine, 1995; Levin, Arluke & Smith, 1981). In these cases, students perpetuate what is expected of them, and the deficiencies only compound themselves through the course of school (Barrick, 2014). Imagine a school career of several years of struggle where you feel like you cannot achieve. Adults in this type of job situation simply find another job. Students do not have that luxury.

What about the student who barely skates by and is disengaged? This student often does not turn in work or does so late and may be found sleeping in class. Teachers may not know the cause of the problem but only think the student is apathetic and lazy. This student may be capable of much more, but may be experiencing some other social/emotional issue or an academic struggle that could be addressed through MTSS. Only by working in these collaborative groups can teachers help to identify the real problems students face and help them reach their potential.

What about the advanced student? Too often, advanced students are not enriched and challenged in schools. Teachers spend so much time teaching the masses and working to catch students up who fall behind that the behaved student who is successful is often left unchallenged. The tragedy here is that these students may never reach their full potential in this environment. Students who are not pushed to excel can end up digressing to the norm of the classroom. Human nature will take over, and students will do what is expected of them, and nothing more (Rist, 1970; Suneal, 2019).

In essence, MTSS is designed to help all students achieve their full potential. The paradigm shift in education is that schools are less concerned about providing education and more concerned with ensuring that students learn. No longer can a teacher say, "Well, I taught the material. The student did not do his/her homework and did not study." Now, teachers have to ask themselves, "Was I effective in teaching the material? Did I meet the needs of the students in my classroom?" Only in an environment when the latter questions are asked will students thrive.

TIERS OF INTERVENTION

In order to effectively use the MTSS framework, educators must understand the three tiers of support that are used to guide a continuous improvement effort within schools. These efforts should be collaborative, systemic, and ongoing. Administrators and teachers must define each tier within their schools based on available resources. See figure 2.1 to understand the three tiers of academic program support and how all students benefit from an MTSS system.

In Tier 1 Interventions, all students are taught the core curriculum with core instructional strategies, whether the core curriculum be Common Core or College and Career Readiness Standards. Tier 1 is the educational foundation and behavioral support for all students, and all students receive the benefits. Behavioral supports can be part of a positive behavior system in which students are rewarded for good behaviors.

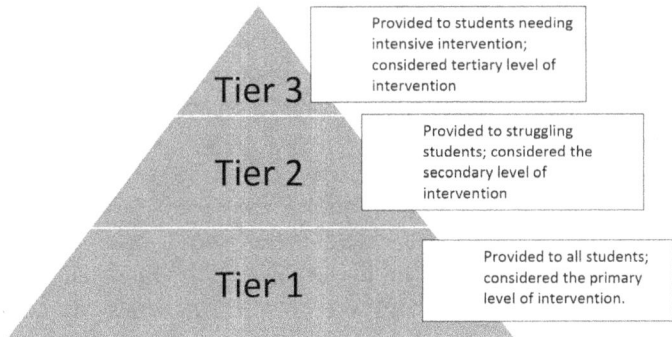

Figure 2.1 MTSS-Tiered Interventions.

These systems can be identified as Positive Behavior Intervention and Supports System, Renaissance Programs, and so on. Many school vendors offer positive behavior systems that schools can adopt. Leadership teams should find one that is right for their schools and their school visions. School community characteristics also must be considered.

Tier 2 Interventions include interventions and preventions that may require small group instruction/counseling, specially designed courses and/or varying instructional materials with progress monitoring. Students in Tier 2 may need on-grade-level and targeted student-level materials to comprehend instruction. These students may also need to be placed in courses that will help bridge educational gaps.

For example, often Foundations of Algebra and Intermediate Algebra are two separate courses taken together that can take the place of Algebra 1. Students who take these courses take two courses rather than the one course of Algebra 1 in order to have more time to comprehend the material. Schools have to be careful with these recommendations, however. The National Collegiate Athletic Association has special rules about some of these courses. Counselors need to make sure that students are able to attain their collegiate goals with the courses they take.

Behavior support groups may also be present in Tier 2, like the aforementioned small group counseling found in Chapter 1. Student mentoring programs can also be considered a Tier 2 support. Essentially, students in this tier of intervention may need a little extra help to access instructional materials as well as behavioral supports targeted to specific behavior deficiencies.

Tier 3 interventions require more intensive, individualized support with small group instruction/counseling, possibly one-on-one assistance, specially designed courses, and specially designed materials with continual progress monitoring. Students in Tier 3 interventions may be placed in an academic learning center at the high-school level or may be pulled for small group reading instruction with a reading specialist in elementary school. Staff providing these intensive interventions need to progress monitor student progress at least every two weeks. In doing so, interventions can be adjusted if needed in order to maximize results. Once students no longer need the intervention, of course, that intervention is stopped.

Tier 3 Interventions, as mentioned, are most intensive and most expensive. Teacher allocation points are required for a number of Tier 3 interventions as well as varied instructional materials. For example, a student in Tier 3 may use an adaptive software program like Achieve 3000 in which materials are provided at the students' reading level, but these materials are on the same topics of the grade-level standards. A plethora of programs exist for students in need of this type of intervention; however, administrators must consult their district policies and budgets in order to determine if the program will work for their schools.

LEADERSHIP

In order for MTSS systems to work, administrators must work with teachers and leadership teams to establish how a student progresses from one level to the next; this is an integral part of developing a student support framework. Interventions need to be defined in the three tiers mentioned above, but what about those advanced students?

Why not develop a Tier 4 so that advanced students also have a path to progress in achieving their full potential? See figure 2.2 for a simple example of the four tiers of academic program and counseling intervention at a school. Of course, schools most likely have spelled out programs that are clear to all stakeholders.

Administrators need to collect data on each intervention regularly to determine if the intervention is helping to achieve the desired result. Additionally, administrators have to acknowledge that fidelity of implementation is often the problem, not the intervention itself. As discussed in the section on teacher support, continued professional development must be provided in order to ensure quality implementation as well as providing observation tools that are in alignment with intervention processes. Teachers need and want feedback; they inherently want students to be successful awkward as they wish the interventions work for students.

PROCESSES

Of course, figure 2.2 does not include all of the classroom-level interventions that are used in addition to academic intervention programs. Again, the process must be spelled out clearly for teachers and guidance counselors to understand their roles and responsibilities. To begin with, leadership teams need to understand the process of developing an MTSS system. Following are the steps that should be taken and questions that need to be answered first.

1. What does an MTSS team look like in the school? Who comprises the team?
2. Are teachers and guidance compensated for their time? If so, how?

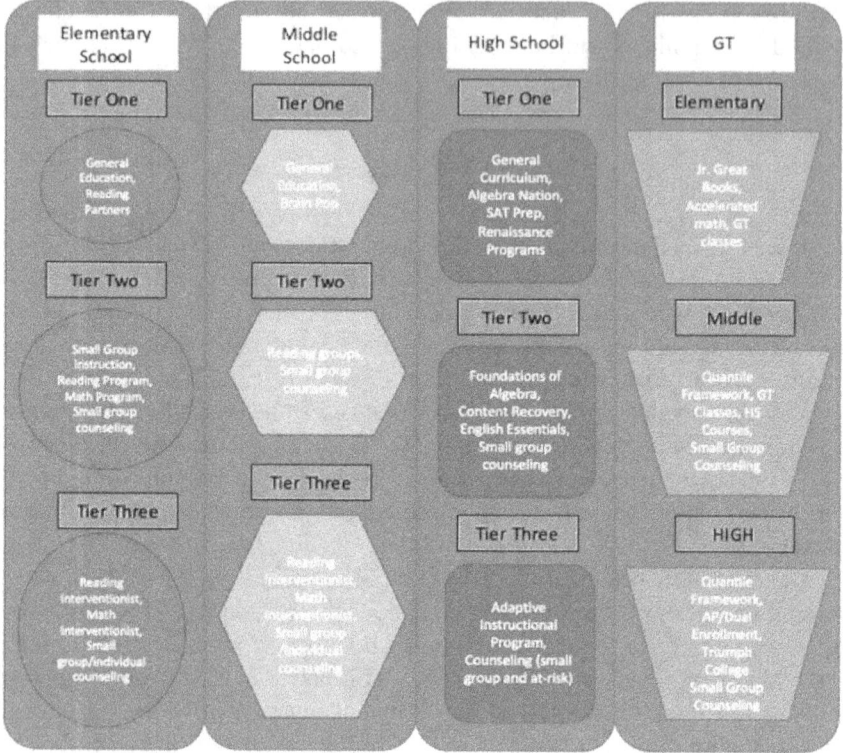

Figure 2.2 Sample MTSS Configuration.

3. When will MTSS teams meet? What is the schedule?
4. What are the red flags used as indicators of needed additional assistance?
5. How many red flags does a student need to exhibit for a referral to an MTSS team?
6. What Level 1 interventions must all teachers implement in the school?
7. How long should a student receive the Level 1 interventions before referring to an MTSS team?
8. How is a student referred to an MTSS team? What is the process?
9. Once referred, what is the process for an MTSS team? How is it recorded?
10. How does an MTSS team follow up on an intervention plan? When do they follow up?
11. What happens if a student works out of MTSS interventions but digresses?
12. What is the parental role in the process?
13. What happens when students are still unsuccessful after all levels of intervention are exhausted?

Thorough planning, answering all of the above questions with a leadership team prior to implementation is crucial for success. Of course, teams may adjust steps in the process, but without a clear process spelled out first, the program will be much less successful. Teachers, as a part of the development, then "own" the process. Rather than having something new rolled out to them, the teachers are the ones vested in the process. Consequently, when teachers share in the problems and the solutions, the solutions have a much greater chance of success (Chandrashekhar & Mini, 2018; Kirk & MacDonald, 2010; Neuman & Simmons, 2000).

Step One

Once school leadership teams have figured out the composition of the leadership team and have developed a shared vision for the team, the next step is to figure out the school-wide Level 1 Interventions that are available to all students. A great, free resource is pbisworld.com, where interventions are spelled out for a number of academic and behavioral concerns. Other companies, like Solution Tree, offer research-based professional development on interventions that work. Administrators have to find what fits the culture and budgets of the schools being served.

Step Two

Red flags have to be determined. How many red flags are needed to qualify for additional interventions? If a student is struggling in one teacher's classroom but is performing well in all other courses, does this struggle warrant an MTSS referral? For this reason, teachers need the opportunity to meet and discuss students they share.

In a high school, time to meet can be problematic because not all teachers will be in proximity of one another or even share the same planning periods. Furthermore, teachers may not even know students they have in common. MTSS leads, who gather the information about student struggles, have the ability to refer teachers to one another if the problem only exists in one class. In these cases, teachers may need to understand the learning styles of a student or the personal struggles a student is experiencing. Teachers talking to one another and sharing ideas equate to better support for students.

Step Three

Leadership teams must determine what happens prior to a referral to an MTSS team to ensure that Level I interventions are being used appropriately. How do teachers record these attempts? Have parents been informed?

Parents do not want the first phone call about their children's struggles to come from an administrator. Too often, parents express concerns that they do not hear from their children's teachers until after the problem is exacerbated, rather than having communication upfront about a potential problem (Baker, 1997). Schools must give parents the opportunity to parent their children first (McKenna & Millen, 2013).

A pre-MTSS form will provide the needed information to the team lead about the number of classes the student is experiencing difficulties as well as the interventions that have been attempted. The lead may determine that additional Level 1 Interventions are needed prior to a referral to an MTSS team due to inconsistent implementations or lack of interventions used. See figure 2.3 for a sample pre-MTSS form that provides needed information to determine next steps.

Step Four

All of the steps in the process must be defined for teachers as to what happens after Level 1 Interventions have been tried and parents have been consulted. This defined program needs to be in writing for reference and ease of compliance. Of course, personnel responsible for components of the process need

Pre-MTSS Form

Student _____ Teacher _____

1. **Concerns** observed (Why is this student a concern?)

2. **Parent Contact** Information (When did you call? What did you discuss?)

3. **Classroom Interventions** (What have you done in your classroom to help this student?)

4. **Changes** due to parent contacts/classroom interventions (Has anything changed due to your hard work and tedious efforts?)

5. **Student Data** (Pull previous data that addresses this issue with the student. Can include, but is not limited to attendance, previous grades, current grades, discipline records, test scores, etc.)

Figure 2.3 Sample Pre-MTSS Form.

Multitiered Systems of Support 29

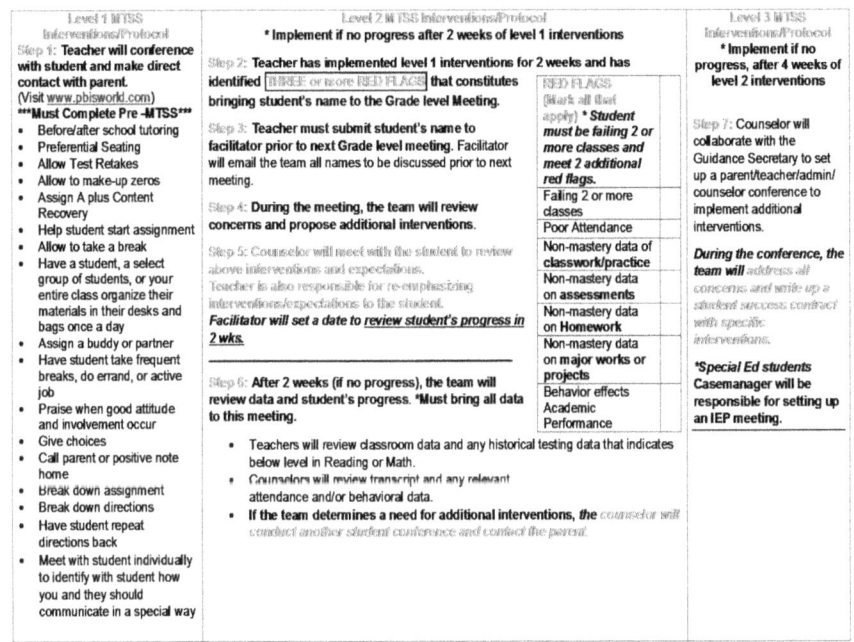

Figure 2.4 Sample MTSS Process Form.

to understand their roles and timelines as well. This planning will take some time, but it will be time well spent. See figure 2.4 for a sample MTSS Process Form.

Notice that this form includes guidance, parents, and administrators as well as some identified Level 1 interventions that must be attempted. Timeframes are included along with data requirements. The data requirements allow the conversations to be held based on factual data, not feelings about students. It is too easy for conversations to be subjective rather than objective when it comes to students. Though feelings about students may be important when understanding student motivations, the data tells a story, too.

Step Five

The process for intervention plans needs to be developed and recorded. Once an MTSS team meets, then what happens? What are the next steps to be taken on behalf of the student? A simple form to outline the intervention plan is needed. Teachers discuss the student's struggles and interventions tried, and then they develop the team intervention plan together.

MTSS
Intervention Plan

Student Name _____   Date _____

Referring Teacher _____   Grade Level _____

Team Members Present:
_____   _____
_____   _____
_____   _____

Interventions Attempted:
_____   _____
_____   _____

Intervention Plan:
_____
_____
_____
_____
_____
_____
_____
_____

Team Lead Signature _____   Date _____

Parents Contacted: YES   NO

Date of Next Meeting:

Figure 2.5   Sample MTSS Intervention Plan Form.

Teachers who may not experience the same struggles with the student share their experiences with one another and also share what they have found to be successful. Every teacher who teaches the struggling student will implement the plan. The MTSS lead keeps a copy of the form as part of the student record and will refer to it in the follow-up meeting. See Form 2.5 as a sample MTSS Intervention Plan form.

Step Six

Follow-up is critical. Once a plan is developed, the team needs to meet again. Did the plan work? What improvements, if any, have been noted. Does the student need an additional intervention? If so, what does that look like for the student and teachers? Forms need to be developed to record what steps have been taken and what steps need to be taken still while in the next level of intervention. If after the designated time for Level 1 through Level

MTSS Follow Up

Student Name: **Grade:**

Follow Up Date:

Interventions that Worked:

Interventions that DID NOT Work:

Follow Up Date:

Interventions that Worked:

Interventions that DID NOT Work:

Next Step	Person Responsible	Due Date	
Historic Data	Referring Teacher		- Grades - Test Data - Attendance - Discipline Reports
Transcript	Counselor		
New Interventions	All teachers, counselor, administration		1. 2. 3. 4.
Conference	Parent/Teacher/Admin/Guidance		Results:
Academic Contract:	Referring Teacher		Attach a Copy
Remove from MTSS?	YES NO		- Any additional referrals needed? - If so, to whom?

Figure 2.6   Sample MTSS Follow-Up Form.

3 interventions there is still no improvement, what are the next steps? See figure 2.6 for a sample MTSS Follow-Up form.

Catch 'em if You can

The purpose of this type of MTSS system is to ensure that administrators and teachers have a clear plan on how they respond when students are not learning or are experiencing difficulties. As stated by Dufour, Dufour, Eaker & Many (2006), "It is disingenuous for any school to claim its purpose is to help all students learn at high levels and then fail to create a system of interventions to give struggling learners additional time and support for learning" (p.106).

It is also important to note that a developed MTSS system is not a series of hoops to jump through before referring students to special education services, as this would also be disingenuous. A developed MTSS system is intended to catch students before that referral ever happens. Schools contain many struggling learners who may never experience that achievement gap that helps to identify them as in need of special services if those students are provided with the appropriate assistance in the beginning.

The principal's role is to guide the staff through the development process. Together, teachers will develop a system far greater than any one person can imagine. The system should be timely, systemic, targeted, and collaborative. Once it is developed, the principal's role, then, is to ensure that teachers are given the time and resources needed to fully implement the plan. Teacher time should be valued, and the meeting times should be embedded in the regular workday, if possible. Additionally, principals should provide professional development for all teachers to ensure they understand the process clearly.

PROGRESS MONITORING

Once the system is developed, progress monitoring is made easier. Multiple data points are available: program performance reports, rates of recidivism, and so on. The forms created along with the data analysis of the program interventions will be critical in determining the success of the system. If a student is dismissed from MTSS, does the student return at a later date? When using a program, such as Achieve 3000 that was mentioned earlier, what do the program reports tell us about the progress of students? Does that progress mirror academic performance? If not, why? What about the fidelity of implementation mentioned earlier?

Principals need to engage in evaluative conversations about the system, not evaluative conversations about teachers. If the system is not getting the desired results, then ask the leadership team for input on changes to the system. With analysis every two weeks within the system, principals should be able to conduct a data analysis on the system every quarter. Adjustments may need to be made, but that is ok. Working toward improvement is a continuous cycle and never remains stagnant, so that is to be expected.

SUMMARY

MTSS systems, or Multitiered Systems of Support, are intended to ensure that all students learn. Only through a systemic design that is school-wide can teachers, counselors, and administrators provide a system of academic and behavioral support for students. This assurance is applicable not only to the struggling student but also to the gifted student. Having a system design that addresses the needs of gifted students helps to ensure that they are challenged in order to reach their full potential.

MTSS System design is based on a three-tiered intervention model. Tier 1 intervention is available to all students in a school and is considered the core curriculum and core instructional strategies. Tier 2 is for those students who are falling behind and may include some specially designed courses or software programs and materials as well as small groups. Tier 3 is more intensive with small group, one-on-one assistance, more individualized materials and resources, and so on. Tier 4 may be designed to address the needs of gifted students.

MTSS design is a multistep process that includes identifying agreed-upon red flags, team members, team leads, meeting times, Level 1 classroom interventions, meeting processes, record keeping, and so on. This process needs to be well thought out and designed prior to implementation. In the design, thought should be given to how a student is referred, what constitutes a referral, and how teams plan for interventions, as well as the follow-up protocol.

Administrators should progress monitor the effectiveness of any specialized programs, such as purchased software, to ensure effectiveness of expended funds. Additionally, administrators should also progress monitor the results of the MTSS system and the process itself. Adjustments may need to be made to improve impact.

A PIECE-AT-A-TIME

- What is an MTSS system?
- What are the three tiers of intervention?
- What could be a fourth tier of intervention? Why is it needed?
- What are red flags, and why are they important to an MTSS system?
- Describe the steps in developing an MTSS system.
- What is a principal's role in an MTSS system?
- How do you progress monitor MTSS systems?
- What types of forms are needed in an MTSS system?

REFERENCES

Assor, A., Kaplan, H., Kanat-Maymon, Y. & Roth, G. (2005). Directly controlling teacher behaviors as predictors of poor motivation and engagement in girls and boys: The role of anger and anxiety. *Learning and Instruction, 15*(5), 397–413.

Baker, A. (1997). Improving parent involvement programs and practice: A qualitative study of parent perceptions. *School Community Journal, 7*(1), 9–36.

Barrick, K. (2014). A review of prior tests of labeling theory. In: Farrington, D. P. and Murray, J. (Eds.), *Labeling theory: Empirical tests* (pp. 89–112). New Brunswick, NJ: Transaction.

Bartusch, D. & Matsueda, R. (1996). Gender, reflected appraisals, and labeling: A cross-group test of an interactionist theory of delinquency. *Social Forces, 75*(1), 145–176.

Center on Response to Intervention at American Institutes for Research. (2014). *Response to Intervention Glossary of terms.* Washington, DC: Author. Retrieved from http://www.rti4success.org/sites/default/files/CenterOnRTIGlossary.pdf

Chandrashekhar, U. & Varghese, M. (2018). Impact of teachers leadership competency on students learning achievement. *Journal of Humanities and Social Sciences, 9*(3), 512–516.

Damico, J. & Augustine, L. (1995). Social considerations in the labeling of students as attention deficit hyperactivity disordered. *Seminars in Speech and Language, 16*(4), 259–274.

Dufour, R., Dufour, R., Eaker, R. & Many, T. (2006). *Learning by doing: A handbook for Professional Learning Communities at work.* Bloomington, IN: Solution Tree.

Kirk, D. & MacDonald, D. (2010). Teacher voice and ownership of curriculum change. *Journal of Curriculum Studies, 33*(5), 551–567.

Levin, J., Arluke, A. & Smith, M. (1982). The effects of labeling students upon teachers' expectations and intentions. *The Journal of Social Psychology, 118*(2), 207–212.

Liu, J., Bartholomew, K. & Chung, P. (2017). Perceptions of teachers' interpersonal styles and well-being and ill-being in Secondary School Physical Education Students: The role of need satisfaction and need frustration. *School Mental Health, 9,* 360–371.

McKenna, M. & Millen, J. (2013). Look! Listen! Learn! Parent narratives and grounded theory models of parent voice, presence, and engagement in K–12 education. *School Community Journal, 23*(1), 9–48.

Neuman, M. & Simmons, W. (2010). Leadership for student learning. *Phi Delta Kappan, 82*(1), 9–12.

Ray, R. (1970). Student social class and teacher expectations: The self-fulfilling prophecy in ghetto education. *Harvard Educational Review, 40*(3), 411–451.

Suneal, K. (2019). Reconsidering organizational habitus in schools: One neighborhood, two distinct approaches to advanced placement. *Harvard Educational Review, 89*(1), 109–131.

Wlodkowski, R. (1978). *Motivation and teaching: A Practical Guide.* Retrieved from ERICDatabase (ED159173) NEA.

Chapter 3

Mentoring Programs

One of the greatest values of mentors is the ability to see ahead what others cannot see and to help them navigate a course to their destination.

—*John C. Maxwell*

The word "mentoring" indicates that a more experienced or successful individual helps to guide and counsel a less-experienced individual or someone in need of assistance. Additionally, the assumption is that if caring adults are available to assist young people, the young people will become caring, successful adults as well (Scales & Gibbons, 1996). This assumption is fair and accurate; however, it is important to note how the mentor relationship is established within the family scope.

When children are younger, they look to their parents and teachers for guidance and support as students compare themselves to others during these years (Erickson, 1950); therefore, mentoring programs should include the parents so that contradictory messages are not received by the students. As students age, they look less to their parents, and in fact, feel that their parents do not understand anything. Peers become the most powerful influence as teens try to form a sense of self (Erickson, 1950).

Mentoring programs, at this stage, may offer separate programs for parents. Mark Twain said it best, "When I was ten, I thought my parents knew everything. When I became twenty, I was convinced they knew nothing. Then, at thirty, I realized I was right when I was ten" (Twain, n.d.). Mentoring programs aim to help support the vision and missions of schools by supporting students through their transitions, but parents' roles must be considered in all types of programs.

SCHOOL-BASED PROGRAMS

School-based mentors can come in more than one form. From a single trusted adult, to guidance counselors, to school psychologists, to small groups—school-based programs can be very effective in helping students navigate social/emotional issues as well as improve perceptions of school (Kuperminc et al., 2019; Slicker & Palmer, 1993). Students who are at risk need mentors the most, and the results of mentoring programs with this student population have been very positive, especially for males (Jekielek, Moore, Hair & Scarupa, 2002; Portword & Ayers, 2005; Raposa, Rhode, Stams et al., 2019). So, what do these programs look like?

Elementary students view mentors as quasi-parents. A mentor, at this stage, is an individual who helps those students understand their worth and abilities. The teacher plays a critical role in this self-evaluation and can serve as a powerful mentor. When young adults are often asked about an influential figure in their lives, they often refer to some elementary teacher who made a lasting impact. Guidance counselors can perform the same function in this setting.

Because students in elementary schools are more than likely with one teacher most of the day, formal school-based mentor programs are rarely established. However, the challenge for teachers is to find time to talk to students on such a personal level when they often have nearly thirty students in a class. For this reason, guidance counselors are often used to teach small groups of students during an exploratory or elective period. These exploratory classes are useful, especially when a developmental curriculum is used, such as set forth with the ASCA National Model standards.

Wouldn't it be helpful, though, if teachers and parents were educated about the ASCA standards as well? Imagine teachers, counselors, and parents all singing the same tune in reinforcing the mindset standards that impact how students feel about themselves. These feelings about one's self impact a student's academic work, most certainly. A belief in one's ability directly impacts one's effort. What about the behavioral standards that develop learning strategies, self-management skills such as grit and persistence, and social skills (ASCA, 2014)?.

Parents, especially, need to understand how their interactions impact student self-perceptions, and this is often not the case. Children can be programmed by their parents without even knowing it. This programming can be positive; however, for those that experience a more difficult home life, a mentoring program can serve to combat that negative programming. Therefore, a strong mentoring program, especially for at-risk children, needs to include a parent education component.

This parent component needs to include more than just a monthly handout that is sent home with students. Schools should personally invite these parents to attend educational sessions in order to better support their children. Who better to send the invite than the classroom teacher? Not only will the impact be beneficial to the students but also to the parents in building trust with the school system. Parents of at-risk children likely have trust issues with schools. Presenting a common front in developing students is powerful and helps to build trust in the community, which in turn provides more support for schools.

Middle-school students, who are trying to figure out where they fit in, need school-based mentoring programs as well. Not only do guidance and small groups have an impact, but one must remember that teachers and parents still leave indelible marks on students at this stage. Therefore, the same types of education programs need to exist as mentioned in the elementary-school program section.

Middle schoolers are an anomaly, in that they want more independence but still need and crave the guidance and support of adults. With changing bodies, defining peer groups and access to more risk-taking behaviors, middle-school students need more guidance than is typically provided. Therefore, neglecting mentoring programs with parental educational components at this stage is disadvantageous.

Programs should be geared toward educating teachers and parents on the same ASCA standards as mentioned above but focus more on the self-management and social skills, since middle school is the time when students really interpret the world around them and how they fit into that world (Piaget, 1952). That is to say, students are finding to which groups they belong and start to share the same values as the group. Therefore, students need mentoring and guidance to help them see all of the options that are available to them and the ramifications of the choices they make.

A formal school-based mentoring program in middle school can be scheduled as an activity period in which students discuss social issues and problems they face with a trusted adult. Students at this age need to learn the coping skills for peer pressure and self-management skills to set their own course. Additionally, these mentoring sessions should also include goals for the future. Even though most middle-school students live for the here and now, they need to be working toward a future plan at all times.

Students need to understand that the decisions they make in middle school can impact decisions made for them in high school, such as course selections and peer identification. Tweens have to understand how short-term goals help to build attainment of long-term goals. These goals need to be set and monitored. Guidance in these matters can definitely have a positive impact on future opportunities, especially when students are helped back on track if they lose sight of the goal.

Middle-school parents as well as their children are sent mixed messages too often from schools. Middle-school students do not want their parents around as much, but they need their parents the most at this age. As a student, it is no longer socially acceptable to be seen hugging your parent when you get dropped off at school. Ew! So, parents try to give their children some space to grow and learn; however, schools need to keep parents in the loop as to what obstacles and potential risks their children face.

As a result, parenting sessions should definitely be included in a middle-school mentoring program. Together, the school and the parents can help support students in a way that is less inhibiting for students while maximizing support. Singing the same tune is very important at this stage of development as well. Students at this age do not want to admit they need help, but they do. A concerted effort between school and home allows students to maintain some independence and confidence while receiving the assistance so sorely needed.

As high-school students gain more independence from their parents with activities and personal freedoms, such as school clubs/sports, driving and dating, the peer influence is the strongest influence at this stage. School-based mentoring programs should be focused on self-management and career goals. Students are nearing the end of their required schooling journey, and the next steps can be scary. Without guidance, these students may not realize their full potential post high school. Let's face it, teenagers are not known for being the most responsible and organized humans. Guidance and assistance are still needed at this stage.

Students graduating from high school often are asked to give advice to students just entering high school. That advice most often is to take your first year in high school seriously, to study and make the grades necessary for college and career readiness. Grade point averages count when considering college choices, and they are hard to improve once established. As such, senior high-school students most often express regret over their freshmen academic years.

For that reason, ninth grade is a critical transition year for students. Parents often think that their children are in high school and are becoming independent. Students often perpetuate that philosophy, because they do not want their parents to hover or even be present; however, it is far from the truth. Consider a ninth-grade student as an inch-taller eighth-grade student.

Parents need to be educated about this transition year and its importance. Not only are students beginning the grade point average race, but they are also getting involved in the school through clubs and activities. The social ramifications of high school can impact the academic performance of students. Helping students stay organized and focused is a big part of this transition year, and parents need the help in supporting their children. Parent education components can assist in this endeavor.

High schoolers continue to need mentoring beyond ninth grade, in that they are trying to figure out what comes after high school. Mentoring programs for these students should focus on college and career readiness with self-management skills, as well as social skills to deal with peer pressures. This exposure to peer pressure increases as students gain independence through the ability to drive vehicles. At this time, students spend more time with peers than parents and family members. These students are at risk of being subjected to and participating in some very risky behaviors without fear of consequence.

In fact, teens often suffer from the "It won't happen to me" syndrome. However, with social pressures that are hard to imagine about body image, acceptance, drugs and alcohol, sex, social media, and so on, teens are processing information about themselves at lightning speeds, more than the prior generations ever imagined. Social media is largely responsible for the increase in teen depression as students are exposed to material that is not always appropriate, to include cyberbullying (Hoge, Bickman & Canter, 2017; O'Keefe & Clark-Pearson, 2011).

For these reasons, parents need to continue to be educated on how to support and communicate with their teenagers. Many parents do not know how to communicate effectively with their teenagers and are left scratching their heads in frustration. Also, some parents display behaviors that teenagers would be advised against in a mentor program. Therefore, school-based mentoring programs are left to address these issues in a non-judgmental way that helps teenagers make healthy choices.

School-based high-school mentoring programs can also be scheduled as an activity period. Each grade level should have a different focus as students progress through stages to independence and social pressures, as well as college and career planning. In doing so, students hopefully gain skills that help them make good decisions for themselves and their futures. Parents need to understand the progression of skills to be taught, as well as communication skills for their homes. Parent sessions should be separate from the student sessions in high school because, again, that independence is needed.

A most impactful strategy is keeping the mentor consistent through the four years of high school. Consistency in support is key, as it takes time for trust to be built among teenagers, especially at-risk youth who are customarily skeptical of adults (Rhodes & Spencer, 2005). Therefore, it is important to loop mentors with students. However, if a connection is not made with the mentor and the student, it is important to recognize that misstep and find another mentor for the student. All students should have at least one adult in the building whom they trust and will share information.

BUSINESS AND INDUSTRY MENTORS

Business professionals can serve as wonderful mentors for students for a few reasons: (1) the adult can relate to expectations of the working world; (2) the adult may have similar experiences and can give advice on how to overcome obstacles; and (3) the adult is not an educator or a parent, thus giving credibility to advice. Remember Mark Twain's words. The strengths of an outside mentor program also dictate the program development specifics.

A mentor program that includes business and industry partners needs to be specific in its goals. For example, at-risk students may need a positive role model in the community to emulate when there is not one at home (Hawkins & Weis, 1985) or someone to help navigate the social challenges of being disadvantaged and the negative effects of mass media (Kashani, Reid & Rosenberg, 1989; Koval, 2019). For these reasons, mentors need to be properly trained on the curriculum and matched to meet the students' needs.

The same training that is provided to teachers and students needs to be provided to outside mentors. These mentors need to understand the social and emotional as well as developmental stages of the youth. Additionally, mentors need to understand the obstacles the children face. Honesty is the best policy here. Parents need to understand the benefits of outside mentors as well as the curriculum to be utilized with the students. Only when all parties understand the goals and processes will the program be successful. Singing from the same sheet music is crucial.

Furthermore, outside mentors need to understand the time commitment. Providing a structured time and space is easy for a school; however, mentors need to understand the true time commitment needed to be successful. This time commitment needs to be more than once a month. Students rely on mentors to show up and participate. Once students bond with an adult, they can come to rely on that adult, even though students might not ever admit that fact.

Adult lack of attendance sends a negative message that the student is not important. At-risk youth receive this message enough; it does not need to be compounded by additional adults. Therefore, administrators must ensure that mentors are truly committed. A long-term mentorship program yields better results for the youth in terms of school attendance, better attitudes toward school, and better opportunities post high school (Tierney & Grossman, 1995).

More and more businesses understand the value of mentoring programs. As such, many businesses support school mentoring by allowing employees time to provide the service. These businesses provide the best mentors because the employee is not having to take personal time or leave time to mentor a youth. Educators should seek those industries that understand the value of such a program to build a sustainable mentoring program.

In high schools, business mentors can be found in many forms such as: small groups, one-on-one mentorships, or sponsors of clubs/activities. For example, a business mentor working with a robotics team does more than work on designing and building a robot. The social interactions can be much deeper and on a more personal level; however, the guise of building a robot offers an opportunity that is less threatening or embarrassing to students who want to be seen as independent. Every club or activity in a school could benefit from having business mentors for the group. Imagine the college and career planning that could result from such a relationship.

ALLIANCES

Never underestimate the power of a community alliance, such as a ministerial alliance or civic organizations. In most communities, there are a number of churches and civic groups, such as a Lion's Club, Women's Auxiliary, Rotary Club, and so on. All of these organizations seek opportunities to support the community. What better way to do so than to provide mentors to students. Most of the time, these organizations are not asked. All that is missing is an invitation.

School personnel also must remember that each organization has a limited number of people who can provide the services needed. So, how can the need of the schools be met? Simply put, pooling resources is the answer. With a large number of denominations and churches that exist within communities, if the number of adults who are available to assist are combined, the resource could be quite impactful. See table 3.1 for an example of a ministerial alliance impact.

Table 3.1 Sample Ministerial Alliance Impact

Organization	# of Mentors Available	# of Students Served
Baptist Church	6	18
Presbyterian Church	4	12
Catholic Church	7	21
Pentecostal Church	3	9
Non-Denominational Church	8	24
Jewish Synagogue	7	21
		105 Students Served

If each mentor from the different churches are trained together on the guidance curriculum to be used, and clear expectations are set about student interactions, church mentors are very powerful resources to tap in a community. Not to mention, these mentors have the right heart to work with at-risk youth. Each mentor could serve more than one student. Imagine the at-risk populations that could be served with such an alliance. Training the mentors, of course, is pivotal, along with educating the parents on the program and its goals and objectives. Clear communication between mentor groups and parents will be crucial to breaking barriers along religious lines.

Another type of alliance, as mentioned above, is with civic organizations. These organizations, like a Rotary Club whose motto is "Service Above Self," can be very impactful as well (Rotary International, 2019). Most communities sustain at least one but often more than one civic organization. Pool those resources; educate the mentors and parents on the goals and objectives; and watch the impact grow. Too often, churches and civic groups work in isolation of one another; however, all of these organizations have humanitarian beliefs. Why not combine resources and ensure students receive the collective benefit?

SYSTEMS PERSPECTIVE

How do administrators build these mentoring systems of support? To begin with, administrators need to start by asking. Too often, school personnel wait for a business to offer assistance rather than the other way around. Invite pastors from the area churches to a luncheon at the school and broach the idea. Ask to present a mentoring solution to local civic clubs during their meetings and invite key members for a meeting at the school. The invitation, though, is not enough.

Hit them hard with data on the needs within your buildings, the number of at-risk youth, homeless youth, etc. Reinforce that schools are not asking for funding, just their time. Put faces with the requests. Too often, businesses are asked for money every time they answer the phone, and schools need to understand that time and talent are more valuable than any donation that could be made.

Spelling out the collective impact that businesses can make is often enough for businesses and churches to come together. Individual organizations, again, cannot support the need, but collectively, the impact could be quite large. See table 3.2 for an example of the collective impact on one school.

Additionally, systems need to include time and space for the mentors to meet with the mentees. Blocking time is important. The system of mentors

Table 3.2 Collective Impact

Organization	# of Mentors Available	# of Students Served
Baptist Church	6	18
Presbyterian Church	4	12
Catholic Church	7	21
Pentecostal Church	3	9
Non-Denominational Church	8	24
Jewish Temple	7	21
Rotary Club	5	15
Lion's Club	5	15
NAACP	8	24
Kiwanis	6	18
VFW	7	21
	Total Student Impact	**198**

entering the building and meeting with kids needs to be clear and concise with mentors signing in and out. This record allows for better record keeping of time, and this time component is important when calculating the collective impact.

Not only do the students and schools benefit but the organizations do as well. Each of the organizations has a mission and goals that often relate to the communities in which they operate. In order to keep the organizations active, however, they need to understand the impact. Through understanding, more support is likely to follow.

DATA COLLECTIONS

Evaluations of mentor programs are critical to sustainability, and this includes progress monitoring. Just as businesses do not like giving funds to a school and not knowing how those funds are being used and the impact they have had on the school, the same is true for mentors. Imagine a monitoring system that tracks not only the number of hours spent in schools and the number of student contacts but also the economic contribution. Good evaluation systems allow for this type of reporting as well as reporting on student attitudes.

Economic impact is easily calculated if the schools have basic information on the mentors themselves. A mentor information sheet is a good way to garner this information as well as connect mentors with students who may have shared experiences. The more connections mentors have with mentees, the greater the impact on the students. See figure 3.3 for a sample mentor information sheet.

From this information sheet, school administrators and guidance counselors can pair students who attended the same schools, may share family structures

Mentor Information Sheet

Name _____   Organization _____

Background Information:

Hometown: _____   Schools Attended: Elementary _____
                                                        Middle _____
                                                        High _____

Family Information
Siblings: Circle One

      YES   If yes, how many _____   NO

            If yes, you are the: Youngest   Middle Child   Oldest

Parental Figure: Circle One
    Single Parent   Divorced (see both)   Together   Grandparent

Career Path:
HS to Work   HS to Technical School   HS to 4 Yr College   HS to Military

Obstacles
What obstacles have you faced that you would be comfortable sharing?

Job Information:
Current Position:

Hours Available to Mentor/Days of Week:

Monday	Tuesday	Wednesday	Thursday	Friday

++Estimated hourly rate or salary for your position: _____/hr or _____/yr

++This information will be used to calculate the collective contribution to the school ONLY.

Figure 3.1   **Sample Mentor Information Sheet.**

and their struggles, may share similar histories, and may even share desired career goals. These connections will give credibility to the mentor's experience and wisdom to be shared. The salary information is used to calculate total economic impact only, and mentors need to feel comfortable sharing this information. To do so, they need to understand why the information is needed.

    Traditional business partners who share a donation to a school or a program can easily report to their customers, directors, and communities that they have contributed "x" amount of dollars to the schools. In doing so, these businesses hope to gain more customers and customer support, as the business is seen

Mentor Contribution Calculation Sheet

Mentor Name_____   Organization_____

Month	Hours	Students	Student Impact Hours (Hrs x # Students)	Hourly Rate	Economic Impact (Hrly rate x student impact hrs)
October					
1-5	2	3	6	$20	$120
8-12	2	3	6	$20	$120
15-19	1	3	3	$20	$60
22-26	2	3	6	$20	$120
29-Nov.1	3	3	9	$20	$180
Subtotal	10		30		$600
November					
1-5	3	3	9	$20	$180
8-12	2	3	6	$20	$120
15-19	1	3	3	$20	$60
Thanksgiving					
25-29	3	3	9	$20	$180
Subtotal	9		27		$540
December					
2-6	3	3	9	$20	$180
9-13	2	3	6	$20	$120
16-20	3	2	6	$20	$120
CHRISTMAS					
Subtotal	8		21		$420
1st Semester	27		78		**$1560**

Figure 3.2   Sample Mentor Contribution Calculation Sheet.

as giving back to its community. However, how do mentors from a business report their contributions? It's really simple.

Mentors spend time, and that time is a valuable resource. Administrators need to report mentor hours, the number of students impacted, the number of hours per student, and the economic impact. To calculate the economic impact, multiply the number of hours by the hourly rate. Hourly rates can be computed if the mentor only reports a yearly salary by dividing the salary by 365 days, and then divide that total by 8. See figure 3.2 for a sample calculation sheet.

Keeping these records on each mentor will allow schools to report the number of students impacted by a business, the number of hours spent with

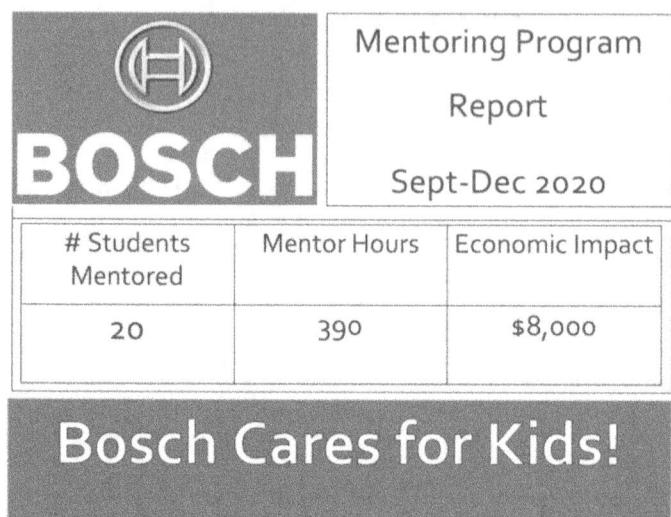

Figure 3.3   Sample Impact Reporting.

students, and the economic contribution in dollars. This information should be shared with the school community and also the community as a whole. See figure 3.3 for a sample impact reporting for an industry.

Businesses cannot always afford to write a check, but seeing the economic impact of the employees' time and talent is very powerful. Communities love to see the number of hours spent and the number of students receiving services as well. This type of data collection is just one data point for success of mentoring programs.

Administrators need to keep these records to report to communities and create support for a sustainable system, but they also need to collect data on the social/emotional impact of a mentor program. According to DuBois, Portillo, Rhodes, Silverthorn and Valentine (2011), mentoring program effects are seen in the softer areas such as emotional stability just as much as are found in the harder areas that are evidenced with data.

SURVEYS

Surveys are a useful tool to understand how people feel about mentoring. Not only do the mentors need to be surveyed but so do the mentees themselves. Surveying mentors about the program, the curriculum, and their perceived relationship with the students will provide valuable information that will help administrators tweak programs to ensure mentors remain in the program. Without asking questions of the mentees, they may become frustrated or

Mentoring Programs

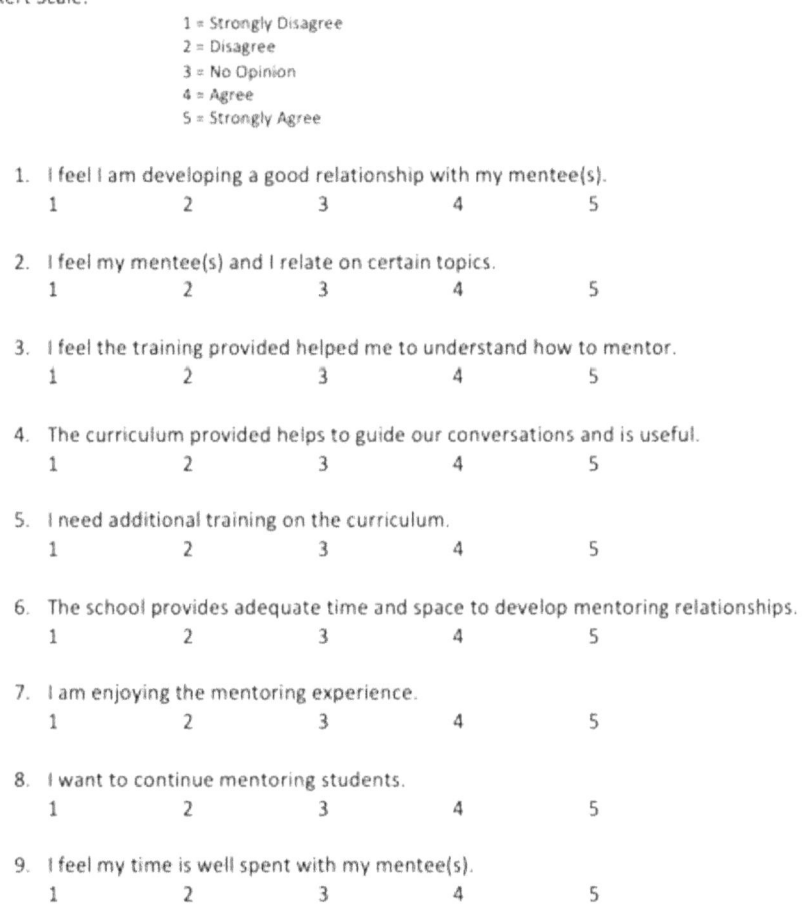

Figure 3.4 Sample Mentor Survey.

disenchanted with a program if they feel that their time is not well spent. See figure 3.4 for a sample mentor survey.

Additionally, mentors may feel they need more training, but they might not necessarily know how to ask for it. The anonymity of a survey allows the adults to answer honestly and let the schools understand their needs as well. Administrators should survey mentors a couple of times a year to ensure the program is running smoothly. This quantifiable data should be shared with the employers as well as in the impact reports.

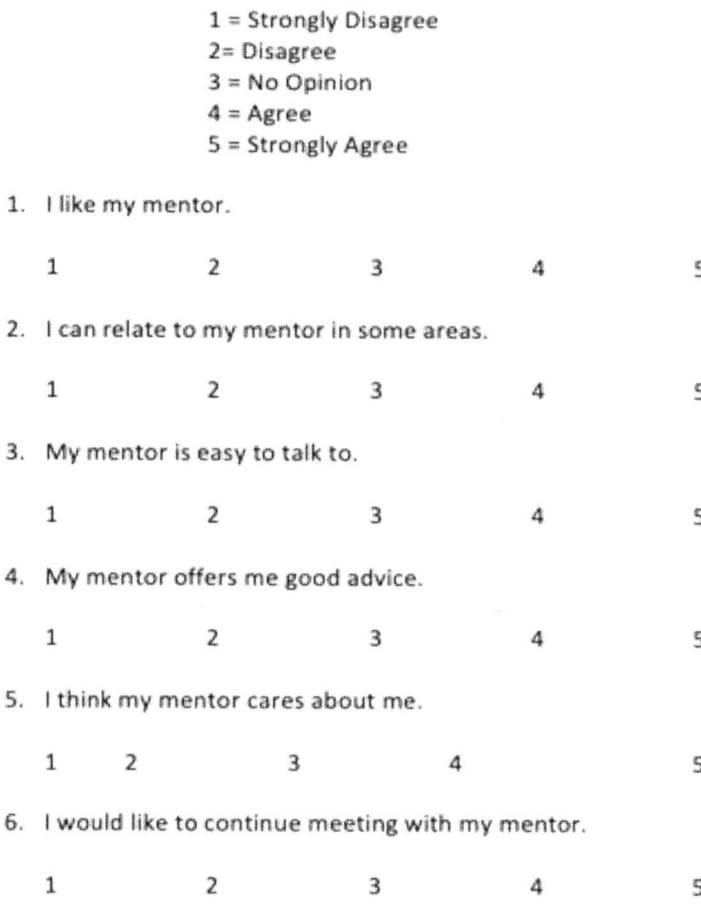

Figure 3.5 Sample Mentee Survey.

In addition to the mentors, mentees need to be surveyed about their perceptions of the program. The perceptions of the students will tell you if the program is making a real impact on the student. Of course, students are known to answer what they think is socially acceptable among their peers. So, mentee survey data needs to be combined with school-based data such as attendance, discipline, and academic performance for each mentee. If school-based data indicators are improving but the mentee reports negative findings on the survey, then the program is still worth pursuing because it is having its desired effect.

These same mentee surveys need to be given a couple of times a year as well. Student perceptions change based on their moods at times. However, relationships take time to build, and the actions of the mentor will speak louder than any words expressed. Regular attendance and real engagement will send a message to a student that the mentor cares. See figure 3.5 for a sample mentee survey.

Again, school administrators need to track school-based data on each mentee; however, another survey may be helpful as well. This survey may be for the teacher or the parent. School leadership teams who work to develop mentor programs need to outline all of the data measures that will be used to evaluate the program at multiple points. These evaluation points need to be created in advance of any implementation monitored throughout the program.

SUMMARY

Mentor programs are valuable when supporting students in schools. At-risk students, particularly, have experienced positive impacts of well-developed mentoring programs. Mentoring programs can come from several sources: school-based mentoring programs, business and industry partners, and community alliances. One of the keys to ensuring a program's success is to include the parents in the education about the program and its implementation. Parent roles are different at the different grade levels, and the parent educational programs should vary to meet those needs.

Mentors need to be appropriately matched with students. Those who have shared similar experiences or share career aspirations may have a stronger impact on a mentee. Using a mentor information sheet will help determine if the mentor and mentee may share any experiences as well as help to determine the economic impact of the program. This level of personal engagement helps to foster school engagement, which positively impacts students (Wang & Fredricks, 2014).

Mentors need training as well. The training should include understanding the developmental phase of the mentee as well as training on the curriculum to be used. All mentors need to have a curricular guide to follow to ensure that students are getting age-appropriate guidance. The National ASCA model provides a strong, appropriate guidance curriculum that is easy to follow.

Mentor programs need to be evaluated for their effectiveness. These evaluation tools and progress monitoring tools have multifunctions. For one, businesses and alliance members love to report their impact on the school community. This reporting is a great marketing tool for businesses, and the publication of such data stirs community support and pride. Each mentor impact can be calculated for the number of students served, the number of contact hours, and the economic impact.

In addition to mentor reporting systems, a mentor program should be surveyed a couple of times a year. These surveys should be designed for the mentor and the mentee as well. The information gleaned from the surveys will inform the administration about the connections being made as well as the effectiveness of the curriculum being used. The information should be used to tweak any program components that need adjusting in order to create a sustainable mentoring program. This survey data is quantifiable and reportable as well.

Lastly, additional survey data may be used to evaluate a program's effectiveness and that survey data may come from mentees' teachers or parents. However, the evaluation components for any program need to be specified, created, and shared with mentors prior to the beginning of any mentor relationship. In addition to survey data, school-based data needs to be monitored to determine a program's impact. School attendance, discipline, and academic performance indicators are often viewed in terms of working with at-risk students.

A PIECE-AT-A-TIME

- What are the three different types of mentor programs?
- What is the value of a mentor program?
- What component of mentor programs should be included that is most frequently forgotten?
- What are the developmental considerations for grade levels when considering mentoring programs?
- How do you measure the impact of business/industry or alliance mentoring economic impact?
- How do you measure the social/emotional impact of mentoring programs?
- What other data measures should be included in the evaluation of mentoring programs?

REFERENCES

American School Counselor Association (2014). *Mindsets and behaviors for Student Success: K-12 college- and career-readiness standards for Every Student.* Alexandria, VA: Author.

DuBois, D. L., Portillo, N., Rhodes, J. E., Silverthorn, N. & Valentine, J. C. (2011). How effective are mentoring programs for youth? A systematic assessment of the evidence. *Psychological Science in the Public Interest, 12*(2), 57–91.

Erikson, E. H. (1950). *Childhood and Society*. New York: Norton.
Hawkins, J. D. & Weis, J. G. (1985). The social development model: An integrated approach to delinquency prevention. *Journal of Primary Prevention, 6,* 73–97.
Hoge, E., Bickman, D. & Cantor, J. (2017). Digital media, anxiety and depression in children. *Pediatrics, 140*(2), 366–380.
Jekielek, S. M., Moore, K. A., Hair, E. C. & Scarupa, H. J. (2002). Mentoring: A promising strategy for youth development. *Child Trends Research Brief.* Washington, DC.
Kashani, J. H., Reid, J. C. & Rosenberg, T. K. (1989). Levels of hopelessness in children and adolescents: A developmental perspective. *Journal of Consulting and Clinical Psychology, 57,* 496–499.
Koval, M. (2019). Psychological characteristics of juvenile delinquency. Series Right, 2(64). doi: 10.32840/1813-338X-2019-2-17
Kuperminc, G., Chan, W., Hale, K., Joseph, H. & Delbasso, C. (2019). The role of school-based mentoring in promoting resilience among vulnerable high school students. *American Journal of Community Psychology, 63,* 1–13.
O'Keefe, G. S. & Clarke-Pearson, K. (2011). Clinical report: The impact of social media on children, adolescents, and families. *Pediatrics, 127*(4), 800–804.
Piaget, J. (1952). *The origins of intelligence in children.* New York: International Universities Press.
Portwood, S. & Ayers, P. (2005). Schools. In: DuBois, D. and Karcher, M. (Eds.), *Handbook of youth mentoring* (pp. 336–347). Thousand Oaks, CA: Sage Publications.
Raposa, E. B., Rhodes, J., Stams, G. J., Card, N., Burton, S., Schwartz, S., . . . Hussain, S. (2019). The effects of youth mentoring programs: A meta-analysis of outcome studies. *Journal of Youth Adolescence, 48,* 423–443.
Rhodes, J. E. & Spencer, R. (2005). Someone to watch over me: Mentoring programs in the after-school lives of youth. In: Mahoney, J. L., Larson, R. W. & Eccles, J. S. (Eds.), *Organized activities as contexts of development: Extracurricular activities, after-school and community programs* (pp. 419–435). Mahwah, NJ: Erlbaum.
Rotary International (2019). Rotary history: Rotary's two official mottoes. Retrieved from https://www.rotary.org/en/rotary-mottoes
Scales, P. & Gibbons, J. (1996). Extended family members and unrelated adults in the lives of young adolescents: A research agenda. *Journal of Early Adolescence, 16*(4), 365–389.
Slicker, E. & Palmer, D. (1993). Mentoring at-risk high school students: Evaluation of a school-based program. *The School Counselor, 40*(5), 327–334.
Tierney, J. P. & Grossman, J. (1995). *Making a difference: An impact study.* Philadelphia, PA: Public/Private Ventures.
Twain, M. (n.d.). Retrieved from http://www.betatesters.com/penn/twain.htm
Wang, M. T. & Fredricks, J. A. (2014). The reciprocal links between school engagement, youth problem behaviors, and school dropout during adolescence. *Child Development, 85,* 722–737.

Chapter 4

Outside Agencies

If a free society cannot help the many who are poor, it cannot save the few who are rich.

—John F. Kennedy

A school is more than an institution of educational services, whether realized or not. Just ask a guidance counselor or teacher. Dryfoos (2005) pointed out that the concept that drives the notion of a full-service community school is that schools alone cannot address all of the problems and needs of disadvantaged children. Yet, schools are charged with achieving learning outcomes for all despite the inequality of resources and family support found among all of the families represented in schools.

Truthfully, schools could help provide additional services not only to the students but to their families and the community at large. In doing so, schools then can become a hub of help and garner much-needed support from the community while working to improve educational performance, but it takes a well-planned, strong leader to do so (Horn, Freeland & Butler, 2015).

NEEDS ASSESSMENT

In order to become well-planned, principals must first undertake a needs assessment of the school and community. This step is an important one because administrators cannot rely on self-reporting of students and families alone. Too often, students will not share their needs and frustrations because they do not want to be perceived as different. Parents often will not share their struggles due to embarrassment. Therefore, a school-based needs assessment can be formulated based on several data points.

SCHOOL-BASED NEEDS ASSESSMENT

To begin, the principal can gather data that is already available. The same information that is used to help identify at-risk students can serve a dual purpose. However, this time, the information is more generalized. See figure 4.1 for data points to consider.

Furthermore, the data on the number of students receiving free or reduced rate lunches needs to be referenced. This is not to say that only students who receive free or reduced lunch rates need services; however, the struggles felt by those living in poverty will provide a broader blanket of services that may address all needs represented in the school and community. Once you have this data point, drill down further. What are the attendance rates of the school? Of those in poverty? If there is a gap between the overall school attendance rates and of those in poverty, that is a signal for intervention, such as parent education, nutrition, and so on.

What about the number of guidance referrals for the school? Knowing the sheer number of referrals is helpful but categorizing the referrals will help school administrators understand the real needs to be addressed (Gilbert, 1957). Categories such as academic struggles, aggressive behaviors, and

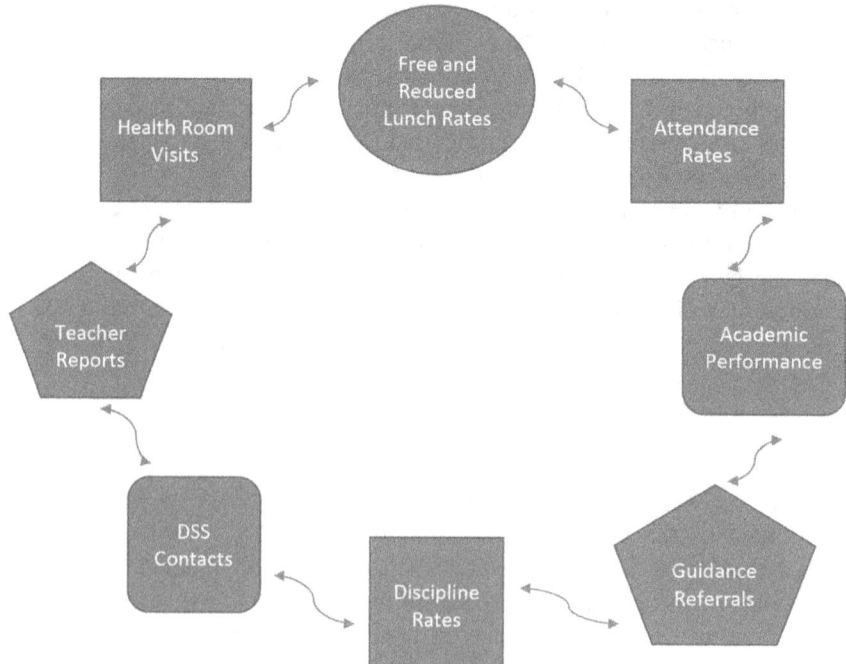

Figure 4.1 Data Points for Needs Assessment.

antisocial behaviors are a good place to start, especially if you disaggregate the data for those who are in poverty.

The same can be said for discipline rates. Not only the number of referrals is needed but the categories as well. Luckily, discipline systems often provide categories for referrals when the discipline is coded in the system. Therefore, reports by category can be pulled easily, and the data can be disaggregated for those in poverty.

Of course, the academic performance of those in poverty is easy to access, but what about teacher reports? To gather this information, teachers need to be asked about the obstacles they see with their students. An administrator most likely will not have this information on all students; it is near impossible. However, teachers are working with the students every day. Therefore, a survey for teachers would be quite useful data to use when developing a program. The survey should be based on identified priorities within your school. See figure 4.2 for a sample survey.

Additionally, agencies such as the Department of Social Services or juvenile court systems often visit schools to check on students. Keeping track of these visits and the underlying causes of the agency interventions are good data points for administrators to use when determining needs. Data is quantifiable and hard to debate. Therefore, each data point mentioned above should be tracked in order to formulate a strong plan for student support.

Health room visits also tell a tale. The number and types of visits can provide useful information to an administrator about the needs of the school. Data from yearly screenings can also help support students and families. If a good percentage of students need glasses, then an outside agency can be contacted to provide services. What about a percentage of students who are under or overweight? Maybe a nutritional program can be useful to help students and families. A school nurse may be the one person a student talks to about issues at home. Never forget to include the health room and the school nurse in all endeavors.

COMMUNITY-BASED NEEDS ASSESSMENT

The struggles of a community become the struggles of a school, as the school is not an island but is representative of the community in which it resides (Taylor & Adelman, 2000). If a community is impoverished, then the educational experiences of the children are impacted. This fact is not questioned. However, schools are charged to ensure that all children are college and/or career ready. Crime rates, family compositions, health factors in addition to poverty all impact communities and, therefore, schools.

Administrators can gather the needed statistical data through local agencies, such as health departments, police departments, and census data. All of

**Teacher Survey
On
Perceived Needs of Students**

This survey is intended to inform administration of the underlying needs and struggles of our students. Please fill out the survey as honestly as possible.

1. Do you have students in your classes that appear sleep-deprived?

    Yes   No   Unsure

2. Do you have students in your classes that appear hungry all the time?

    Yes   No   Unsure

3. Do you have students in your classes that are never prepared for class with materials or assignments?

    Yes   No   Unsure

4. Do you have students in your classes who don't have adequate clothing (weather-appropriate such as coats, shoes, wears dirty clothes to school, etc.)?

    Yes   No   Unsure

5. Do you have students in your classes that have poor hygiene?

    Yes   No   Unsure

6. Do you have students in your classes that appear withdrawn?

    Yes   No   Unsure

7. Do you have students in your classes that are drawn to violence, either demonstrated in their work or by exhibiting aggressive behaviors)?

    Yes   No   Unsure

If you have answered YES to any of the questions above, please make guidance referrals for these students immediately. If you have answered UNSURE, please take note of the students in your classes and make any referrals necessary.

Figure 4.2   Teacher Survey of Student Needs.

this information is public information and is, thereby, accessible. This collection of this data also opens doors for collaboration with the agencies that keep the data. Multiple data points should be considered.

Single parent homes face challenges that a two-parent family home may not encounter, such as work schedules and the various needs of the children.

This may also impact transportation needs for extracurricular activities and medical treatment. What about children that are raised by their grandparents? Though loving, grandparents may not fully understand the educational demands of children today, much less know how to help them. Parent education programs are needed to help fill the gaps for these families.

Crime rates definitively impact a school's culture. If children do not feel safe to come to school or feel safe while in school, learning will not be optimized. Therefore, understanding the crime rates in your community can help administrators plan to ensure an environment conducive to learning. Parents/guardians need to understand the challenges schools face with rising crime rates, as well, so that schools and guardians can work together to ensure child safety.

Health factors that plague a community can also directly impact educational experiences for children. If a community's statistics show that the number of pneumonia cases is on the rise, then early medical treatment options may be a factor and that impacts educational programs for parents as well as children. Educational programs may also include screenings and medical services provided within a school system, such as free dental and vision care. Additionally, information on drug use, teen pregnancies and the like can also be obtained from agencies that can help direct the formation of programs catered to the needs of the community.

The compilation of the data from within the school and from the community is the first step. The next step is to build a network of community agencies that can assist your population. A network that works together, rather than in separate silos, has a greater impact. Schools can be the catalyst for the network to work together for the sake of the children.

RESOURCES IN YOUR COMMUNITY

State Agencies

The first step to establishing the network is to identify all of the agencies within your community that may offer support. The standard state agencies include the ones from which you gathered data: Department of Social Services (DSS), police departments, and health departments. Presenting a collaboration between the agencies and your school is a powerful practice.

If crime rates are up, the police department may help police the student routes to and from school. Parents may volunteer to monitor the routes as well. Additional police presence may be needed at extracurricular events in order for students to feel safe. If the community is experiencing a rise in a particular health issue, inviting the health department in to educate students and parents may prevent further spread of the issue. Parents may need help with dealing with their difficult teenager, diminishing cases with DSS. The list can go on and on. Agencies love the invitation for collaboration because the focus is on prevention rather than reaction to a crisis once it has already occurred.

Local Agencies

Other agencies within your community that are more local include civic organizations such as a Rotary Club or Lion's Club. These groups' purposes are to serve the community. Inviting representatives from these organizations to understand the challenges facing your school may redirect their efforts to you. The Rotary Club may provide assistance with classroom materials, such as dictionaries and equipment. Additionally, the Lion's Club may work with the school to provide some after-school care and tutoring.

Agencies like the United Way, the American Red Cross, and the Boys and Girls Club of America have local offices in most cities. However, communities have their own local organizations as well. For example, in Charleston, SC, there are over twenty-five agencies listed on one website as nonprofit organizations focused on family support and assistance ranging from Kids on Point to Be a Mentor to WINGS for Kids to Woodwind Family Services. Additionally, there are over thirty agencies to fight poverty and hunger as well as health issues. Each agency has a mission that may align with your school's needs.

Compiling a list of resources with contact information with the mission of each is, again, the first step. Reaching out to establish a connection and collaboration is the next.

See table 4.1 for examples of local neighborhood agencies in Charleston, SC. This list was generated from a simple Google search, and with the advent of the internet, more resources are available for schools and families to utilize.

NEIGHBORHOOD AGENCIES IN CHARLESTON, SC

Relationships

Each agency can become inundated with requests for assistance as the need can outweigh personnel, and funds are not unlimited. Therefore, it is very important to establish strong relationships with these agencies. Invite agency representatives in for a luncheon and share the school data with them. Show them the impact they can make on children with wraparound

Table 4.1 Neighborhood Agencies in Charleston, SC

Agency	Focus	Contact
Be a Mentor	Mentoring Youth	
WINGS for Kids	Social Emotional Learning	
Woodwind Family Services	Children At-Risk of Abuse	
Kids On Point	Under-resourced Neighborhoods to provide academic and athletic enrichment	
HALOS	Assistance to abused and neglected children and their caregivers	
Destined Shades of Purple	Mentoring young women	
Dream Center Clinic	Free medical clinic to underserved populations	
Closing the Gap in HealthCare	Medical education for underserved populations	
Favor Foundation	Provide food, clothing, and referral services for job placement	
Humanities Foundation	Provide housing, financial relief to avoid eviction or loss of utilities	
Low Country Food Bank	Feed the needy	

services provided in the school. Collectively, the impact they can make on your school is immeasurable. However, singularly, the impact is one case-at-a-time, if at all.

To further develop the relationships, invite them back with quarterly updates on support provided. This includes man hours, resources expended, and the number of children and families impacted—all of the quantitative data. What more, the qualitative data is the data that pulls the heartstrings. Administrators and teachers should share stories of how children's and families' lives have been improved and how that has changed the educational experience for children.

By providing the quantitative and qualitative data, the agencies are more likely to provide more support or at least remain consistent with their levels of support. Humanitarian-based agencies want to know their efforts and resources are put to good use and are having an impact—bottom line. Without the follow-up to include data, businesses are often left to feel that their money goes into an anonymous cause and may not have any impact at all. Think about how many times you hear the phrase "throwing money at a problem."

Another way to build relationships with the agencies is to publicize their support and impact. Of course, identifying information on specific students and families is forbidden. However, using that same quantitative and qualitative data to sing their praises shows appreciation of efforts. This is a highly motivating practice, and it encourages the community to become a stronger supporter of the agencies in terms of community support and financial commitment.

A Systems Approach

A system is needed so that teachers, counselors, and administrators know who to go to for the problems presented in the community and the school. Once the needs assessment is done, a guide should be developed with all of the agencies and community support mechanisms identified with contact information. In doing so, time is not wasted, and immediacy of response is dictated. Teachers need to know who to turn to once a problem is identified rather than trying to work with a student singularly because meeting the needs of all students can be overwhelming at best.

Therefore, the guide should include the "if a student . . . then you contact" scenarios. Educating the teachers on the needs assessment will help them understand the issues facing the community and the students. If teachers do not have experiences with similar obstacles, it is harder for them to relate to their students. Also, if they do not fully understand the gaps that exist in the school as well as the needs, they cannot possibly address them.

Provide professional development on the ramifications of the challenges facing the community so they can better understand and build relationships with their students. Too often, teachers can wrongly attribute student behaviors and think students lazy or lack the value of an education rather than attribute the behavior to the real problems facing students.

This professional development should also provide teachers with coping mechanisms and tools to engage students in the classroom. It is one thing to understand a student's issues, but it is another to help a student work around them. Consequently, teachers need strategies in their tool belts to help address the myriad of issues that face youth today.

Administrators should also develop educational programs in the school for students as well as families based on the needs assessment. Partnering with agencies to provide preventive educational programs may diminish negative impacts. Most important is to include parents in these programs. As mentioned earlier, parents may not feel comfortable coming to the school; so, administrators may have to take the programs to the parents via local churches, community centers, and the like. Additional collaboration is needed with these institutions to make it happen, but the extra efforts are worth the time and can help build community capacity (Haig, 2014).

A schedule of educational programs needs to be developed and included in the guide for teachers and counselors. In doing so, staff can not only enlist extra assistance when helping students but also share the program information in a timely fashion. When everyone is working off of the same script, the message is louder and clearer.

Once the guide is established and professional development is provided, administrators should monitor the effectiveness of the system. To do so, the same school data used in the needs assessment needs to be revisited at regular intervals. Is academic performance improving? Are student discipline rates down? What about guidance referrals? The data provided as updates to agencies should be included in this progress monitoring. How many referrals are being made to outside agencies? Is the school providing adequate support for students and families? If not, the system may need to be altered or more assistance enlisted.

SUMMARY

The importance of enlisting the services of outside agencies as part of the system of student support cannot be understated. Students today face more challenges than many can imagine. These challenges are found in the school communities at large. As such, schools can serve as a center of support for the community that can help equalize underserved neighborhoods (Williams-Boyd, 2010).

In order to provide the proper services, one must first conduct a school and a community needs assessment. Discipline, attendance, academic performance, and health room visits need to be examined and categorized in order to identify issues. Additionally, teachers need to be surveyed in order to get a full picture of the student body's needs. Community agencies such as DSS, police departments, and health agencies should be contacted to gather community data. All of the data combined can provide an administrator with a full picture of the community the school serves.

Once that picture is illustrated, administrators should then seek to gather information on the agencies within the community that are available to offer assistance. A chart should be created to include the various agencies, their foci, and contact information. Agency representatives should be invited to understand the school data in order to develop a strong collaboration of wraparound services for students and families.

The agencies should receive reporting on their efforts to include quantitative and qualitative data, which serves to motivate further support. Information on the impact of the collaboration should be publicized and shared with the community as well. Agencies need to feel appreciated and supported, too.

Lastly, school administrators should work to provide professional development to all school staff on the challenges in the community as well as to provide strategies to help students learn around the challenges. Staff should also be provided a guide of scenarios and who to contact for additional assistance because a collaborative effort is more effective than a singular one when providing student support.

A PIECE-AT-A-TIME

- Prior to enlisting outside agency support in a student support system, what is the first step?
- What are the types of school data used in a student support system?
- What are the types of community data used in a student support system?
- Give examples of state and local agencies in your community.
- How can the information be organized for all concerned?
- How can you support your community agencies?
- What types of professional developments are needed?
- How do you progress monitor outside agency support and its impact?

REFERENCES

Dryfoos, J. G. (2005). Full service community schools: A strategy – not a program. *New Directions for Youth Development, 107*, 7–14.

Gilbert, G. M. (1957). A survey of "referral problems" in metropolitan child guidance centers. *Journal of Clinical Psychology, 31*(1), 37–42.

Haig, T. (2014). Equipping schools to fight poverty: A community hub approach. *Journal of Educational Philosophy and Theory, 46*(9), 1018–1035.

Horn, M. B., Freeland, J. & Butler, S. M. (2015). *Schools as community hubs: Integrating support services to Drive Educational Outcomes*, Vol. 3. Washington, DC: Brookings Institution.

Taylor, L. & Adelman, H. (2000). Connecting schools, families, and communities. *Professional School Counseling, 3*(5), 298.

Williams-Boyd, P. (2010). Breaking bonds, actualizing possibility: Schools as community hubs of social justice. *Forum on Public Policy Online,* Vol. 2010, No. 4.

THE CULTURE SYSTEM

Culture is the final system in the analogy of building a schoolhouse. If you recall, the first step is to lay the foundation with a systems perspective. The second step is to frame the outer walls or the system of curriculum and instruction, for curriculum and instruction are the basis of teaching and learning. The vertical supports are the teacher support systems, with the horizontal supports as the student support systems. Teachers and curriculum and instruction help to support students. Lastly, all of these systems help to build a school culture. So, it stands that the final system is the culture system or the roof of the schoolhouse.

Culture can be created and should not be an accident. Administrators should be purposeful when creating culture because cultural change is the hardest change. It takes time and patience. However, neglecting culture is a fundamental mistake. If an administrator focuses solely on academics, culture suffers and academic achievement will not be maximized. If an administrator focuses solely on culture, then academic achievement will suffer. Essentially, an administrator must focus on all systems simultaneously to maximize results, and culture is a critical system that is frequently not planned as much as it should be.

Chapter 5

School Culture System

The heart and soul of school culture is what people believe, the assumptions they make about how a school works.

—*Thomas Sergiovanni*

One must understand culture in order to establish it. The culture of a school is the mindset in how a school operates, the norms, and expectations. This is why administrators must understand that their every action works to establish culture. What if that administrator's actions conflict with existing cultural norms? Establishing a culture is much easier than changing one, and administrators must understand that just like any other change, cultural change is a process and will not happen overnight.

The desired school culture must be planned over time, and consistency has to exist in the visioning of a school. Leaders must be strong in their convictions, and their actions must match their convictions if cultural change is expected. Inherently, people find change difficult. Change pushes people past their comfort zones. However, to a culture that may have existed for years and years, proposed cultural change is like a virus to the existing culture (Gruenert & Whitaker, 2015). Naturally, viruses are attacked from within; this is why the effectiveness of cultural change will depend on the strength of the administrator and his/her convictions.

GROWTH MINDSET

Lots of different types of school cultures exist out there, but in order to establish an effective school culture that can keep up with the ever-changing demands, one must not only understand but also adopt a growth mindset.

Carol Dweck (1999) understood that in order for students to achieve their potential, they must look beyond their fixed mindsets (what their abilities are believed to be by others) to focus on a growth mindset (what students believe they can achieve). In essence, teachers and students alike must believe that more can be achieved by all, just as they must understand that the achievement is gained through experiences, both cognitive and emotional (Darling-Hammond et al., 2019).

This growth mindset must be established in students through interactions with teachers, administrators, and families. Teachers and administrators must believe that students can achieve more than they traditionally have, and students must be given the opportunities to do so. According to Rosenthal and Jacobson (1968), students will achieve what is expected of them. If teachers believe that students can achieve more, students will rise to the challenge. This self-fulfilling prophecy has been proven time and again (Brophy, 1983; Brophy & Good, 1974; Walker & Graham, 2019), but for some, it is the most difficult concept to grasp.

Maybe the difficulty lies within the teachers themselves. In order for teachers to understand inherently that students can achieve beyond their demographics, poverty levels, and the like, teachers also must have a growth mindset when referring to themselves. Teachers need to continue to learn and grow in their professions. In order for this to happen, teachers need to value goal setting and professional development and not be threatened by not always having the answer.

Teachers must believe that they can and should learn and grow in the teaching discipline to include instructional strategies, classroom organization, and so on. Maintaining status quo will not improve a culture and create a growth mindset. This enhanced teacher growth can help meet the needs of all students as well as provide more opportunities for students to learn. Moreover, teacher growth mindsets are not created without an administrative growth mindset.

PRINCIPAL ROLE

In order for teachers to strive to improve for the sake of their children, administrators must do the same for the sake of their teachers and students. The principal's role in creating a growth mindset is critical and instrumental in producing any change. In fact, the research base on leadership demonstrates clearly the powerful relationship between leadership and school development (Hallinger & Heck, 1998). Not only does the principal need to create a shared vision but the principal must also walk the talk. Identifying the real obstacles within a school and finding solutions to tackle them is the hard part.

Too often, attention is given to the symptoms of a problem and not the problem itself. This is difficult for teachers to grasp. Imagine the conversation about students' grades and progress. Can you hear the conversation revolving around student apathy, lack of studying and doing homework? Those student behaviors are symptoms of the larger problem. It is a harder to pill to swallow that the problem may be in the lack of dynamic instruction or relevance of the learning.

Therefore, the principal must be willing to lead the hard conversations with teachers and recognize that the school support may be a part of the real problem. Principals have to be willing to work harder than anyone else in the building to provide the best instructional support system for teachers, where failure is viewed as an opportunity to learn rather than a measure of value. Students deserve the best schools have to offer, as expectations can predetermine student outcomes (Gentrup, Lorenz, Kristen & Kogan, 2020).

Schools preach that failure is an opportunity for students to learn, and teachers must continuously adjust instruction to promote student learning (Starratt, 2003); the same principles should be applied to teachers with opportunities to learn without penalty. Teachers have to trust this is true in order for them to be willing to change. That is why the principal must talk the talk and walk the walk.

This growth mindset with teachers cannot be stand alone. This mindset must permeate a school's climate, which then impacts the community's beliefs. The principal has to sing the same tune with the school district, school, and business community. This messaging must remain consistent and permeate all aspects of the school. Consistency, again, creates belief.

Principals have to remember that students, teachers, and families all share the same values. All parties want students to be successful and achieve beyond school. However, the roads diverge based on experiences; beliefs are shaped by experiences. Student, teacher, and parent experiences may not have been the most supportive or creative. As such, the beliefs these stakeholders share may not align with the vision of the school.

It is the principal's job to consistently provide different experiences so that the belief structure will change to mirror the shared values. See figure 5.1 for an illustration of the ripple effect that can be created.

DISTRICT ROLE

How does a principal operate in a district that may be perceived as not sharing the same growth mindset? Too often, principals complain that the school district in which they work expects to see the same programs across schools, that one shoe must fit all. Sometimes, this is the case, but it is not the problem.

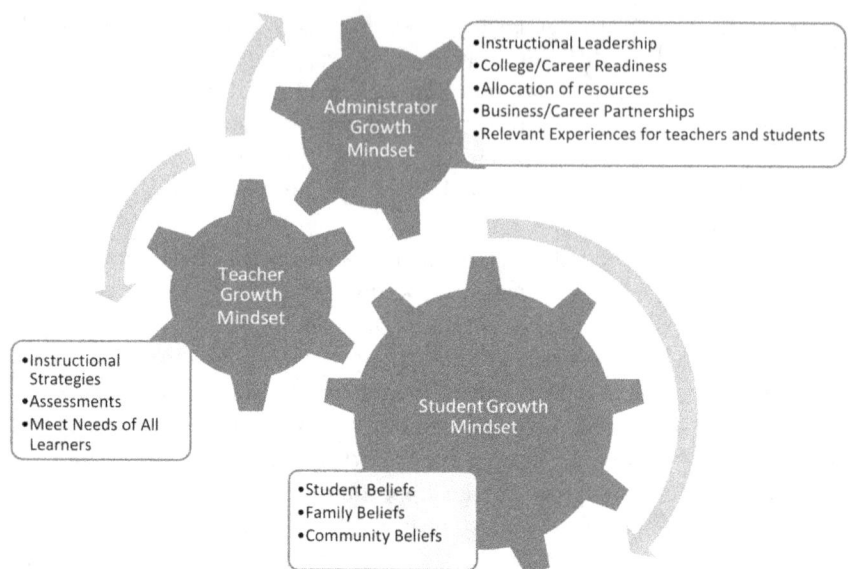

Figure 5.1   Effects of Growth Mindset.

Principals must understand that they have autonomy within their buildings to create a culture within their walls, separate from the district's.

School district office staff are charged with seeing patterns across a district. These patterns help determine the professional development needs across the district where the resources expended have the greatest impact. However, each school may have additional needs. Therefore, it is incumbent upon the principal to recognize the difference and fill the needs within his/her school. Principals cannot expect that a district office will provide all of the needed support. It simply is not possible.

Therefore, principals must take charge of the growth mindset within their own buildings. Principals cannot wait for a district office staff to fulfill their individual school needs and complain when it doesn't happen. Too often, principals are waiting for the central office staff to provide support, and these principals have missed the boat.

When principals work with teachers to identify the needs within their buildings and build programs based on the individualized needs of that building, teachers see the principal as a resource and a leader. All principals may not be strong in instructional leadership, meaning they may not be able to lead the staff development; however, all principals can and should ensure that teachers get the help they need. Principals should also participate in that professional development with teachers so that the administration can serve as a real resource, understanding what the teachers are expected to do.

The district role, in these cases, is to support the principal. Conversations need to be held with district staff, explaining the needs of the school based on data. Plans should be shared so that district staff can support the principal in his/her endeavors. More times than not, district staff are more than happy to support the individual efforts of principals when they see the principals taking the initiative to improve their schools based on data and best practices research. Data and research are hard to argue with. Principals have to remember, you have no right to complain if you are not willing to do the work yourself.

COMMUNITY ROLE

The community's role in this cultural change endeavor is important and often overlooked. Creating a real growth mindset, as stated earlier, is difficult because it may require cultural change. Administrators must remember that this change and its impacts are heard loud and clear in the community as well as within the school and district. If these stakeholder groups do not understand the plans and the "why" of the plans, negative feedback is sure to follow, making the principal's job that much harder.

Therefore, principals must understand that the school community also needs to understand the plans for the school and why the plans are changing in order to provide support. If the principal has teachers in the building who do not want to change, lack of community support can be dangerous for that principal. Imagine the following scenario:

> A new principal comes into a school with a culture that is not conducive to change. Teachers are happy to maintain status quo because they have established routines and work flow is manageable. Parents support the school generally because they feel that if their children are passing, the teachers are doing their jobs. However, students in this school are performing well below state standards, but the parents and community members do not understand this fact, because their children are advancing to the next grade and eventually graduating. Teachers do not want to implement the changes proposed by the new principal, because they are happy with the teaching routines and curriculum they have always taught. These teachers talk about this new principal in the community with disdain, and parents listen. Because the parents think the teachers are already effective, parents' voices along with teacher voices are heard at the district level. Within a year or two, the principal is moved or demoted due to ineffective leadership.

The principal in this scenario undervalued the impact community support has in the building and in attempts to implement a growth mindset. Unfortunately, that mistake was costly.

In this scenario, the principal's job is to garner this community's support for the change that is needed. The principal must truly explain to the parents and students where the students' academic standings really are within the state. This can be difficult for people to grasp, but the data tells the story. Then, without missing a beat, the principal must explain that their children deserve better; they deserve better in the classroom which will result in better opportunities outside of the classroom.

To achieve this growth, the principal must share the growth plan with the community. In doing so, community members will support the change efforts and growth mindset. Remember, they share the same values, but their beliefs are based on their experiences. Principals must provide them different experiences. In doing so, teachers who do not want to change will feel the pressure to change because the community is depending on them to do so.

FEEDBACK

In any growth endeavor, it is important to provide data-driven feedback to all stakeholder groups. Principals should inform their teachers regularly on growth measures and celebrate the small successes. These celebrations provide accolades and motivation to continue within the building. Incentives and public recognition of success serve as magnified motivators for teachers.

These same celebrations and feedback should be shared with the district staff. As the district office staff was made aware of the growth plan initially, sharing data on successes and challenges will help the central service staff provide additional support and motivation. Keeping central office apprised of successes and progress also affords the principal more autonomy in branching out. Remember, data tells the story, and the goal is student learning for all kids. No one wants to be the person to stop progress.

As the community support was initially garnered for the change needed, the community needs to have progress reporting on the successes along the way. Not only will this feedback provide support and motivation for students to continue to achieve in the school but will serve the same purpose at home. Parents want to be proud of their children's successes, and students crave the praise from their parents. Consequently, students can then be motivated to work harder so they can continue to receive praise.

This community feedback and progress reporting can also serve the same motivating purpose for teachers. When the community can congratulate and thank a teacher for helping their children succeed, teachers are motivated to continue to grow and learn. Teachers crave the same acknowledgment of hard work from their school administration, colleagues, and community members. Hence, a growth mindset must include the community in its development.

MOVING PARTS

Administrators must understand that the work of creating a growth mindset is hard work and requires many moving parts. These parts include not only creating a shared vision and community support but also a strong needs assessment backed by data. This needs assessment will underscore the need for change as well as the access points for change.

However, a principal cannot do this work alone. For this reason, teacher leadership in the building is essential. Teachers inherently want to feel valued within their institutions. Just like teachers crave acknowledgment and praise for their hard work, many teachers also seek leadership roles within their schools. Administrators should think intently on the school organization and how the work of the school can be shared with teacher leaders. As stated multiple times, the job it too big for one person, and the collective intelligence and work of the whole is far greater than the one.

Therefore, administrators should strategically think about how the school organizational structure can be created to support the work that needs to be done. When teachers are involved in the planning and decision making, their ownership drives the outcomes. Meaning, when teachers are invested in creating the plans, they work harder to ensure that the plans are successful. Consider the strategic organizational structure that currently exists within your schools and how that structure can be altered to maximize impact and support.

Each school may have committees such as a Leadership Team or Data Teams; however, there are many other committees to consider. Who does the research and developing plans for the school? Who is in charge of analyzing the data to create a professional development plan? Who is in charge of the emotional supports for the staff? Who works on the community feedback piece? The point is that teachers who share in this work are empowered and motivated to continue to improve. The principal is one person who can help lead the charge; however, one person cannot do the work alone in creating a culture. That has to come from within the organization and permeate every pore.

Each committee must understand its charge in supporting the vision of the school and how measures are progress monitored to provide feedback to one another. In figure 5.1, committees report back to the leadership team. The flow of work is organic, in that it moves both up and down the structure. The principal should be knowledgeable about all of the work of the committees but not lead all of them. Being a part of the leadership team is imperative, but being the chair is not.

The principal's role is to provide guidance and feedback on proposals where teachers may not understand policies, financial obligations, local politics, and so on. Principals can make suggestions that result in decisions made by the teachers. The point is teachers own the work, not just the principal. In doing so, more is accomplished and teachers feel valued and invested.

The first step in creating this workflow is to establish the types of committees needed and their functions. Something like the committee structure presented in Putting the Pieces Together: A Systems Approach to School Leadership's Chapter 9 (Westberry, 2020) allows the principal to work with the leadership team to identify the needs of the school in terms of the work to be done as well as the collaborative ownership of the work. This type of leadership requires a skillset among principals that can identify faculty strengths and cultivate them. Training may need to be provided by the principal in order to establish group norms and methods of work. However, the rewards are well worth the work!

How each committee functions and reports progress is important to establish before any work begins. This can be the charge of the leadership team to establish. Progress reporting and work expectations with established parameters need to be planned upfront so that there is no wasted time. Time is one of the most valuable resources a teacher has at his/her disposal, and that time should be honored and respected.

Timelines for progress reporting should be established so that each committee will unequivocally know the work of each other's committees. In doing this, committees are motivated to stay on track with the work. In essence, teachers provide motivation for each other. Also, this progress monitoring reporting allows for celebrations within the school, the district, and the community, as mentioned earlier.

EVALUATION

Too often, administrators are evaluated on the academic outcomes of a school. Understandably, new accountability measures have placed increased pressure on principals to meet certain benchmarks. The same is true for teachers. Because of this pressure, school districts are infamously known for dropping a program and finding a new one with a promise of better results. Everyone is looking for that panacea that will cure the ills in school. However, the data presented does not always paint the full picture of a program's worth.

Evaluations of programs should include evaluations of the processes and fidelity of implementation. Arthur and Blitz (2000) stated that programs must be implemented with fidelity to the original model in order to preserve the behavior change mechanisms that first made the model effective. Meaning, if schools do not adhere to the original model of a program, the results will lack.

This evaluation includes the evaluation of systems in your school. Does the committee structure work? Is the work getting done that needs to get done?

Are the norms being followed? In order to create a growth mindset, administrators must evaluate the culture system itself, just as one would evaluate a curriculum. Sometimes systems need a tweak here or there to get the operation running smoothly again.

If one is not looking, the damaging effects of a system not running efficiently can directly impact students and teachers. This damage can create a negative culture and counteract the desired culture you are trying to create. Therefore, the committee structures need to be evaluated as well as the output of the committees. This type of evaluation is underutilized in schools and can create the best results. In these situations, teachers will tell you what they need to be successful if they are only asked. In addition, evaluation systems need to be created prior to a committee beginning its work.

Just as teachers are asked to plan with the end in mind, administrators should do the same in all endeavors. Creating a growth mindset culture is not different. Principals need to understand what that mindset looks like and how it can be not only created but also evaluated before structures are put in place. In doing so, teachers understand the expectations of each group and can fulfill them with confidence.

So, what would an evaluation of a committee look like? Evaluation forms can be quite simple, but they should be used regularly to provide feedback to the groups. If evaluation feedback is not utilized regularly, such as twice a year or each quarter, time may be wasted. Remember, time is a most valued resource. See figure 5.2 for an example of a simple evaluation form.

SYSTEMS APPROACH

To create a systems approach to creating a culture, or a change in culture, administrators must look at each aspect of the culture in the school.

1. What is your vision for your school? How is it communicated and to whom?
2. Do teachers believe their students can and will learn?
3. Do teachers feel a sense of responsibility for their students?
4. What do students think about learning? Do they think they can achieve and excel?
5. What does the community believe? What experiences have they had with the school in the past?
6. What systems does the district have in place? What support is available?
7. What is the current culture of the school? What is the climate?

When answering each question, administrators can identify the steps needed in order to create a growth mindset. Each area has to be addressed

1st Quarter Data Team Evaluation

Responsibility	Needs Improvement	Met	Exemplary	Notes
Meets when scheduled				
Utilizes reporting forms consistently				
Roles are defined and adhered to				
Analyze Benchmark Data each quarter and report				
Report trends found in school to leadership team				
Compare data to end of year assessments				
Cross reference with at-risk group of students				
Make recommendations				

Celebrations	
Recommendations	

Figure 5.2 Sample Committee Evaluation.

strategically so that teachers feel support by the school, district and community, and students feel the same. Principals should plan backward by establishing committees utilizing teacher leadership to analyze each of these factors and then determine next steps. Remember, the job is bigger than any one person.

Once committees are done with analyzing the current status of culture, these same committees can work to identify the gaps from where the school operates to the desired vision for the school. That is the first step. Then, teacher leaders will work to identify strategies and support needed to achieve the desired vision. Often, these strategies overlap a school's strategic plan but that strategic plan is often void of evaluation and celebrations. These necessary steps cannot be forgotten. Additionally, the community support piece is often overlooked as a necessary first step.

SUMMARY

School culture defines how a school operates, what it believes as an institution. It is important for administrators to develop a growth mindset among students and teachers. This growth mindset overcomes a stagnate identification and combats the status quo often found. If students have been conditioned to believe they can only achieve to a certain level, that is all they will achieve. The self-fulfilling prophecy is not only true for students but for teachers as well.

The principal's role in establishing culture is vital. The principal must be viewed as a resource and support for all of those he or she is wanting to affect, to include students, staff, and the community. Knowing the existing culture is fundamental to begin the work of changing the culture to one of a growth mindset. A needs assessment of the existing culture should be completed to fully understand where the gaps may lie.

The administration of a school must not ignore the culture of the community. Remembering that a school community shares the same values but may have different beliefs based on their experiences is instrumental in changing the conversation. If parents and community members know precisely how a school intends to support their children, administrators garner more support from the community and the teaching staff.

Teachers not only need to share a vision for the school but also have to possess the tools necessary to achieve it. In doing so, administrators would be wise in soliciting the assistance of teacher leadership in the building in building a culture. When teachers feel invested and trust the leadership to support them, teachers will achieve more than a single person can accomplish alone.

However, teacher teams need to own the vision of the school and understand how their work will be valued and appreciated.

The systems approach to establishing culture should be examined and strategically planned. Utilizing teacher leadership and evaluation of outcomes in addition to processes will help administrators affect real change in a school and community. District office staff will support what is clearly understood and reported.

A PIECE-AT-A-TIME

- What makes up a school's culture?
- What is a growth mindset culture?

- How does a principal garner the support for change in the community?
- How do principals garner the support of cultural change with a teaching staff?
- How can you organize school committees to impact cultural change?
- What are important components to remember when establishing these committees?
- What is the importance of evaluating committee work?

REFERENCES

Arthur, M. W. & Blitz, C. (2000). Bridging the gap between science and practice in drug abuse preventions through needs assessment and strategic community planning. *Journal of Community Psychology, 28*(3), 241–255.

Brophy, J. (1983). Research on the self-fulfilling prophecy and teacher expectations. *Journal of Educational Psychology, 75*(5), 631–661.

Brophy, J. & Good, T. (1974). *Teacher-student relationships: Causes and consequences.* New York: Holt.

Darling-Hammond, L., Flook, L., Cook-Harvey, C., Barron, B. & Osher, D. (2019). Implications for educational practice of the science of learning and development. *Applied Developmental Science, 24*(2), 97–140. doi: 10.1080/10888691.2018.1537791

Dweck, C. S. (1999). *Self-Theories: Their role in motivation, personality and development.* Philadelphia, PA: Taylor and Francis/Psychology Press.

Gentrup, S., Lorenz, G., Kristen, C. & Kogan, I. (2020). Self-fulfilling prophecies in the classroom: Teacher expectations, teacher feedback, and student achievement. *Learning and Instruction*, 1–17. doi: 10.1016/j.learninstruc.2019.101296

Gruenert, S. & Whitaker, T. (2015). *School Culture Rewired: How to define, assess and transform it.* Alexandria, VA: ASCD.

Hallinger, P. & Heck, R. H. (1998). Exploring the principal's contribution to school effectiveness: 1980– 1995. *School Effectiveness and School Improvement, 9*(2), 157–191.

Rosenthal, R. & Jacobson, L. (1968). *Pygmalion in the classroom: Teacher expectations and student intellectual development.* New York: Holt.

Starratt, R. J. (2003). Opportunity to learn and the accountability agenda. *Phi Delta Kappan, 85,* 298–303.

Walker, S. & Graham, L. (2019). At-risk students and teacher-student relationships: Student characteristics, attitudes to school, and classroom climate. *International Journal of Inclusive Education*, 1–18. doi: 10.1080/13603116.2019.1588925

Chapter 6

Support

If you want to change the culture, you will have to start by changing the organization.

—Mary Douglas

School principals need to understand first and foremost that they will only be successful with community support. This community can be defined as the school community, the district community, and the business community. Each area needs to be explored and developed so that the principal can maximize effectiveness for the sake of the students and teachers he or she serves.

SCHOOL COMMUNITY

Recognizing that a school is more than an institution of learning is the first step. Schools can become the hub of a community quite easily, and frankly should be. Schools do not operate in isolation of the community but in conjunction with the community. So, if the community is facing obstacles, so will the school. In fact, the community is an important vehicle for child learning and development (Simon & Epstein, 2001). Often, the school is the vehicle for solutions to problems or can help find a way to alleviate the problems a community faces.

Parents and Students

A principal's challenge is to ensure that a community inherently knows that he or she is there to assist and truly has the best interest of students at heart. Parents need to know that administrators are invested in the success of students and care about them as individuals; parents must trust administrators (Adams & Forsyth, 2007; Byrk & Schneider, 2003). In order to achieve this, an administrator has to first be visible. This visibility is imperative (Dinham, 2005; Khalifa, 2012), but showing up is not enough. Teachers are often told that attending events of their students makes an impact on their students. It does. The same is true for principals, but the impact is made on the students as well as the parents.

Attending events opens the door for discussion outside of the regular school setting. Some parents are too intimidated to enter a school and make an appointment with a principal. However, a principal can approach a parent of a group of parents at an athletic event, fine arts event, and so on and initiate the conversation. Breaking down the barriers that some parents may face can make a principal approachable.

Additionally, parents notice if a principal supports students and so do students, for that matter. Attending the events, some or all of them, and interacting with students is vital. It is not enough to just be seen. Principals need to take the time to talk to students, cheer them on, and provide leadership when facing obstacles. As a community leader, principals are a vital part of the community solution (Green & Gooden, 2014).

Think of the school organizations which exist but do not get the attention that say a football team does. What are those organizations in your school? What clubs exist within your school? Visit them all. Robotics competitions and band competitions are full-day events and often require travel; as such, they are rarely attended by administrators. However, principals miss out on a fantastic opportunity to connect with students and parents!

What about the Junior Reserve Officer Training Corps (JROTC) programs in schools? JROTC students have only a few competitions a year; however, JROTC can serve over 100 students in a school or more. Though these events do not draw big crowds, other than the parents of the students competing, these are examples of exemplary opportunities to connect with students and parents and garner support while demonstrating it.

Do not limit yourself to competitions, either. Visit the chess club, book club, or any organization you have in your school where students can be found. Attend an art event and chat with parents about the talent found in the school and the program itself. Talk with students about their inspirations and what the art program needs in the school. In essence, the more support you give, and the more engaged you are, the more support you receive in return. Principals do not have to just be visible, but they have to be present. Students and parents know the difference, and you will be amazed at what students and parents notice.

What about the issues facing the community? Administrators must understand the community's needs and try to support its families through the struggles they may face. School organizations often engage in volunteer experiences. Think of the chorus, National Honor Society and the student council in your schools. It seems that school organizations are always involved in volunteer, community events, which is wonderful!

Students need to learn about the world in which they live and how they have the power to change it. However, each organization knows its singular impact. An administrator has a bird's eye view of the entire school's impact. This information should be tracked and reported to the community. In fact, it should be celebrated!

If a community is experiencing a particularly difficult or pervasive issue, imagine the impact a school can have if each organization focused its volunteer efforts to alleviate that issue! A school may not be able to solve the problem, but a school can certainly make a dent. Additionally, the community support that results as a visible, concerted effort to invest in the community can be overwhelming. Additionally, students learn the value of civic responsibility and how they can give back and make a difference. What more, trust continues to be built with the school and administration as school activities are aligned with the affective needs of the community.

Principals need to be present and support these community service efforts as well. Whether students are coordinating a food drive, car wash, or adopt-a-highway day, imagine the impact it makes on the community to see a picture of the principal boxing food, washing a car, or picking up trash. The principal is the role model for the students and the community. Administrators need to make sure the message they are sending is the one that they want to be received.

So, how can a principal manage all of the visibility and engagement while maintaining any kind of work-life balance? This is the burning question of the day. As a principal, you are always "on." That should be expected. However, administrators need to weave in their family time as well. The best bet is to schedule everything in advance. Each organization should be able to provide the principal a schedule of events for a school year. Ask for it.

Coordinate athletic events, clubs, and competitions on a master calendar, like a master schedule. The same is true for community events and service opportunities. See table 6.1. Additionally, administrators need to schedule all of these events with the administrative team of a school. All members should be required to contribute their time, as the team approach also sends a message to the community. Plus, there are other benefits.

It is important that the school be represented at these events, even if the principal is not the representative. By sharing the experiences with the administrative team, the principal has the opportunity to be visible at more events but does not necessarily have to be there from beginning to end. "Pop-in's" can be effective as well, as long as the principal is visible and present.

Table 6.1 Typical Principal Calendar of Support

Monday	Tuesday	Wednesday	Thursday	Friday	Saturday	Sunday
1 Volleyball @ 6:30 (AP) (Drop In) Student Council Meeting 4-5 Rm. 201 (P) Drama practice 4-6 (Drop In) Band Practice Volleyball Practice	2 Cross Country 4:30 State Park (AP) (Drop In) Robotics Practice 4-6 (Drop In) Band Practice Volleyball Practice	3 Chess club Rm 410 (Drop In) BETA Club Rm. 312 4-5 (Drop In) Robotics Practice 4-6 (Drop In) Band Practice Volleyball Practice	4 Volleyball @ 6:30 (AP) JV Football game @6:00 (P) Choir Practice 4-6 (Drop In) Drama Practice 4-7 (Drop In) Band Practice	5 Varsity Football @7 (P/AP)	6 Band Competition 9-9 @ Columbia (P) Cheer Competition 9-4 @ Charleston (AP -Drop In) Student Council Car Wash @ AutoZone @8-12 (AP) (Drop In)	7
8 Drama Practice @4-6 Cross Country @4:30 Home (P) Volleyball Practice Band Practice	9 Volleyball @ 6:00 (P) Robotics Practice (Drop In) Drama Practice Band Practice	10 Book Club Lunch (P) Robotics Practice Band Practice Volleyball Practice	11 JV Football 6:00 Away (AP) Volleyball @6:30 (P) Choir Practice Drama Practice Band Practice (Drop In)	12 Varsity Football @7 (P/AP)	13 Cross Country Meet @ 8:00 a.m. (P) SAT Testing @8-1 (AP)	14

15	16	17	18	19	20	21
Drama Practice @ 4-6	Volleyball @ 6:00 (AP)	Cross Country @ 4:30 (P)	JV Football @ 6:00 Home (P/AP)	Varsity Football @7 (P/AP)	Robotics Competition @8am-9pm (P/AP)	
NHS Meeting@ 6-7 (P)	Robotics Practice	Robotics Practice	Volleyball @6:30 away		JRTOC Marching Competition @8-2 (P)	
Volleyball Practice	Drama Practice	Band Practice (Drop In)	Choir Practice (Drop In)			
Band Practice	Band Practice	Volleyball Practice	Drama Practice			
			Band Practice			
22	23	24	25	26	27	28
Drama Practice 4-6	Volleyball @6:30 (AP)	Cross Country @ 4:30 (AP)	SIC @5:30 (P)	Varsity Football @7 (P/AP)	Drama Production @7-9 (P)	Drama Production @2-4 (AP)
NHS Meeting @6-7 (P)	Robotics Practice	Robotics Practice	PTSA @6:30 (P)	Drama Production @7-9 (AP)		
Volleyball Practice (Drop In)	Drama Practice	Band Practice	Volleyball @6:30 away			
Band Practice	Band Practice	Volleyball Practice	Choir Practice (Drop In)			
			Drama Practice			
			Band Practice			

Notice that in table 6.1, the principal (P) has delineated which events he or she will attend as well as which events will be covered by assistant principals (AP). Additionally, the calendar shows which events the principal plans to drop in. It is important to note that the drop in's often occur when the principal already has a scheduled event. Other times are scheduled so that when the principal is not on duty, the principal can drop in events and still get home for needed family time.

Scheduling of administrative support should be purposeful. Note, in this schedule, the principal attends a volleyball game the second week of the month and also attends a volleyball practice. This type of presence shows the students that the principal is invested beyond supervisory needs. Drop in's for band practice, drama practice, or robotics practice allows a principal to connect with the students when they are not in competition mode. Students see that as real support. Don't think these students will not tell their parents about the visit, because they will, especially if the principal engages with the students.

When you look at the calendar, you will see that the principal is working three to four nights a week, as well as on weekends. Of course, once trust is established, the principal may scale back to three nights a week, including weekends. However, this will depend on the size of the administrative team and the needs of the community. The point is, principals need to expect to spend this proportionate time with their school community each week. This is the job of a principal to garner real school community support. In order to get support, you have to give it.

Booster Clubs

Booster clubs are organizations that are created in order to support, or boost, a particular student group, such as athletics, drama, band, and so on. These organizations are comprised of parent volunteers who have a vested interest in being engaged with their children's school and interests. They fundraise to support the activity, expend funds to support the activity in the way of equipment and materials as well as travel, and they act as a real voice in the community. Booster clubs help to raise social capital as well as financial capital (Fritch, 1999).

Do not underestimate the power of a booster club; however, be cognizant of the dangers within a booster organization. Because these organizations act as fiscally independent agents of the school district, the same finance policies do not apply. Booster organizations keep separate bank accounts and can spend funds without district approval. Therefore, it is vitally important that principals are connected with their booster organizations.

Even though a school district does not have oversight when considering booster finances, a principal can and should exercise monitoring processes.

A principal should require that booster organizations submit monthly statements that outline expenses that should coincide with monthly reports to parents in the booster organization. In doing so, the principal can ensure that monies are being expended as the booster charter is intended. Additionally, principals should require annual proof of the tax-exempt filings with state agencies in order to retain legitimacy as a fundraising vehicle.

Working with booster parents in achieving the shared goals for a program facilitates increased support for the principal within a school with parents and students as well as in the community. Principals should take the opportunity to report to booster organizations the progress on school goals and strategies employed in the spirit of transparency. Open communication with booster organizations creates extended avenues for feedback and support.

These parents who are active members of booster organizations create their own communication webs that extend to the community. Therefore, parents can advocate for principals and communicate the school's vision and progress in order to reach more of the school community.

Sometimes booster organizations can garner too much independence and can violate rules and regulations that are intended to guide these organizations. This is another reason why administrators have to be aware and involved with booster clubs. Monitoring booster activities in the spirit of support and engagement affords the principal the opportunity to ensure policies and laws are being followed without appearing to be scrutinizing. Booster clubs have to understand that though they stand alone, they only exist with the permission of the principal. According to most state laws, a principal has the right to disband a booster club and remove officers if there is any wrongdoing.

Civic Organizations

Civic organizations, as stated earlier, exist in most communities, such as a Lion's Club whose motto is "We Serve" (Lionsclub.org) or a Rotary Club whose motto is "Service Above Self" (Rotary.org). Civic organizations are designed to improve their communities and the world in which we live, and they are comprised of business professionals in the community that have a servant leadership heart. Additionally, civic organizations often are made up of the real community leaders. Therefore, civic organizations provide a prime feeding ground for school support.

Joining a civic organization as a school administrator is highly recommended. In doing so, your weekly or bi-weekly meetings offer the principal opportunities to communicate about the school's vision, goals, progress, and difficulties. Educating the community leaders on the good things happening in schools allows that positive press to permeate a community. Too often, people only hear the negative. Just watch the local news. However, this communication web with civic leaders is powerful and can combat any negative press that a school may receive. Education and communication is the key.

Additionally, civic groups' activities afford the opportunities for students to collectively support a community cause and spread goodwill in the community. The reverse is also true. Civic groups need to be welcomed in a school to work with the students in their environment. A Rotary Club working with a school's student council on a coat drive creates more positive support for a school and administration than can be imagined. Adults need to see just how great today's students really are instead of just hearing what the local news has to say.

DISTRICT COMMUNITY

The school district's support of a school, or lack thereof, has a tremendous impact on a school in several arenas: funding, programs, and community awareness. This is not to say these two areas are the only ways in which districts support schools; however, school communities do not necessarily see the impacts of the other areas, such as evaluation, curriculum, personnel supports, and so on. Just as a high-school band program needs to understand that no matter how much the students work toward a superior rating at a concert festival, the community does not see all that effort and applaud that success as they do for a great marching band program.

Remember these words: what the community can see, the community is more apt to support. Therefore, in order to secure district support, a school administrator needs to publicly applaud and celebrate the district support of a school as much as possible. In doing so, the district will be happy to return the favor. For example, a school's Distributive Education of America (DECA) student group qualified for national competition, and the district helps fund the travel. Make sure to create a press release on the accomplishment of the students, teacher sponsors, as well as the district for supporting student competitions.

Imagine a school joins a robotics league in middle school, and the district supplies the needed materials for students to learn and build robots, advancing STEM (Science Technology Engineering and Math) education. A principal needs to take the opportunity to publicly praise not only the students and teachers involved but also the district for supporting future STEM leaders. In essence, a principal needs to publicly thank and applaud district support in order to facilitate the collective community.

In public recognition of district support, the school community can extend their support of the school to the district. This symbiotic relationship benefits both a school and a district, and as a result, the community. Too often, schools and districts are viewed as an "us v. them" mentality, and that divisiveness can create tensions in the community. Therefore, it is important to recognize and share support. The benefits extend to all parties, especially the students.

BUSINESS SUPPORT

Community business support can come in a couple of forms. Schools traditionally have enlisted business partners and, in more recent years, academy partners. The break from traditional norms is that the focus has more recently been put on the sharing of a business's time and talent and not just its financial resources. This trend is more powerful than just the ceremoniously writing of a check because students develop real college and career readiness skills from the business representatives, and these representatives have more credibility than the teachers in the students' eyes.

Business Partners

Successful business partnerships benefit both the business and the school. Businesses are more apt to develop a partnership when they realize a benefit as well. Additionally, businesses need to know exactly where their hard-earned financial resources are going and how they impact the school. Too often, businesses are asked to write a check as a partner without necessarily knowing the impact made. For that reason, a few simple rules need to be followed when developing business partnerships:

1. Clearly define the need for the partnership.
2. Clearly specify how funds will be used and their impact.
3. Write a partnership contract that is renewable yearly.
4. Allow the partner to determine the services desired from the school.
5. Measure and report the impact back to the partner.
6. Abide by clearly defined agreements.
7. Evaluate partnership yearly prior to renewal.

These steps may seem simple, but several steps are often overlooked. A business partner likes to share with the community that the business supports the school; therefore, the process is made easier if administrators establish partnership levels. In doing so, businesses can choose their own levels of support, where the funds are expended, and what services they receive in return. See figure 6.1 for a sample business partnership contract.

Business Partnership Contract

In an effort to build strong community support and involvement at (School Name), (Business Name) has agreed to partner with (School Name) for the _____ school year. The following partnership terms are applicable:

(Business Name) will do the following for (School Name):

1. Provide monetary support in the amount of _____ for the _____ activity/organization.
2. Provide supplies and material in the amount of _____ for the _____ activity/organization.
3. Provide discounts in the amount of _____ for the _____ activity/organization.
4. Provide man hours to support the _____ activity/organization.

(School Name) will do the following for (Business Name) at the _____ level of sponsorship.

Platinum Partnership ($2,500 + per year)

1. Advertise on Renaissance Rally T-Shirts with business logo
2. Advertise in school newsletters
3. Advertise on school web site with link to business
4. Submit a press release on partnership agreement
5. Provide a partnership certificate
6. Recognize the business at a partner recognition dinner
7. Recognize the business on a partner recognition public display

Gold Partnership ($1,000 - $2499 per year)

1. Advertise in the school newsletters
2. Advertise on the school web site with link to business
3. Submit a press release on partnership agreement
4. Provide a partnership certificate
5. Recognize the business at a partner recognition dinner
6. Recognize the business on a partner recognition public display
7. Advertise on school marquee

Silver Partnership ($500 - $999)

1. Advertise in a school newsletter
2. Advertise on the school web page with link to the business
3. Submit a press release on partnership agreement
4. Provide a partnership certificate
5. Recognize the business at a partner recognition dinner
6. Recognize the business on a partner recognition public display

Bronze Partnership (up to $499 per year)

1. Advertise in a school newsletter
2. Advertise on the school web page
3. Provide a partnership certificate
4. Recognize the business at a partner recognition dinner

We at (School Name), working in conjunction with (Business Name) agree to the terms and conditions in this partnership contract signed on _____.

_____   _____
Principal   Business Representative/Owner

Figure 6.1   Sample Business Partnership Contract.

As seen in figure 6.1, business professionals can pick the level of partnership they think they can support, and the school provides the public recognition for the partner through various means, such as news releases, web pages, newsletters, business partner dinners, recognition boards, and so on. All of these measures show the partner appreciation for their support, and the business may gain additional patronage or good will within the community.

Business partners can support a plethora of programs such as chorus, Future Business Leaders of America, Parent Teacher Organizations, and so on. However, pairing a business partner with a department is a good idea, too, especially when the partner knows how the money is to be spent within the department. For example, a chemical plant can support the science department, and the monetary donation can be used to purchase science supplies. A building contractor can support the math department in purchasing materials and calculators. Pairing businesses with departments that make sense provide more motivation for partners to engage and write a check.

Other business partners include those that provide discounts to the students, parents, and teachers. For example, a dry cleaner may provide a 20 percent discount to teachers, or a food establishment may provide free meals to a few teachers once a month. This type of discount/partnership should not be undervalued. Teachers love the incentives and appreciation. What about the food establishment that provides free kids meals for those students making honor roll? Remember to include each of these types of partners in your partners list.

Per the partnership agreement, administrators and business partners should meet annually to review the partnership and ensure that all parties are satisfied. During the annual meeting, the terms of the contract should be reviewed as well as the services that were provided to the partner. Additionally, the partner should be given a handout on how the funds or services benefited the school and students. A nice touch is to have students write thank you letters to the partner, recognizing the impact of the support. Providing specifics allows the partner to see the direct benefit of the partnership, and they are then less likely to withdraw that partnership, especially when they see that students directly benefit from the support.

Another key point about business partnerships to remember is that the same businesses are asked for support by multiple schools and school groups and organizations each year. The financial resources allocated to giving can only stretch so far, and businesses get inundated with requests. The best way to address the partnership with the business is to ensure that once an agreement is signed, the school will not ask for additional funds throughout the year. In essence, business partners are placed on a "protected" list. Business professionals like this added bonus because no one likes to say no to giving, but it is often necessary.

Academy Partners

The current K-12 school challenge under the *Every Student Succeeds Act* (2015) is to ensure that all students graduate from high school as college and career ready. This is a big challenge knowing that all raw materials are not the same, meaning students do not come to school with the same experiences and same aspirations. Teachers and administrators work diligently to ensure success for students while in their care; however, success can be defined differently: technical school, college, military, and work. Any and all of these paths will spell success for students, by anyone's standards. However, schools are charged beyond that to ensure readiness for all of the four paths.

More schools have recently turned to career academies to help with college and career readiness of students. Career academies, according to the National Career Academy Coalition (2018), have been in existence for over four decades. In essence, career academies are small learning communities that focus the core curriculum around a career theme. As early as 2011, law makers became involved in this growing trend. In 2011, Florida legislators required each school district to have at least one career academy (Boyd & Gladden, 2013).

In order to support academies, schools have turned to businesses to help. An academy partner can come in many forms, much like a business partner. However, academy partners focus on the career pathway and developing skills in students. For example, an academy partner may brand an academy. In an urban school in South Carolina, the local sheriff's department branded the Law Enforcement Academy. The academy was named after the local municipality: The Berkeley County Sheriff's Department Law Enforcement Academy. To brand an academy, the investment from the entity requires time, talent, and resources.

Additionally, students in this academy receive work-based learning opportunities when they work alongside sheriff's deputies in training and ride-a-longs. Additionally, the local sheriff's department helps fund the materials needed in the course, all while developing a workforce. Career academies can and should help alleviate local workforce development struggles.

ACADEMY PARTNERS

An academy partnership is a mutually beneficial arrangement between a business and a high-school program. Partners commit themselves to specific goals and activities intended to enhance educational opportunities for students and teachers related to the academics of the school.

Partnership Levels

Platinum: Branded Academy. $100,000 of in-kind services and/or funds for the first year and $25,000 of funds and/or in-kind services for four additional years. Memorandum of Agreement required.

Gold: $50,000 of in-kind services and/or funds for the first year and $25,000 of funds and/or in-kind services for three additional years. Memorandum of Agreement required.

Silver: $10,000–$15,000 of in-kind services and/or funds per year. This commitment is made on a year-to-year basis. Memorandum of Agreement required.

Academy Partnership: No established value of in-kind services and/or funds per year. Annual review. No Memorandum of Agreement required.

In doing so, academy partnerships require a commitment beyond writing a check. These partnerships are student-involved. For example, another academy, a business academy, at the same school was branded by a local car dealership. This investment spanned several years, wherein the CEO of the company was often found teaching business classes filled with students, and students were found developing marketing materials for seasonal campaigns. Both the students and the academy partner benefit from the relationship. See textbox 6.1 for sample academy partnership levels.

Non-branded academy partners are valued as well. These partners do not necessarily engage in the largest commitment, but they are still invested in developing career readiness skills. A partner that donates time to develop curriculum and provide student internships and teacher externships (where teachers learn the demands in the field), and the like helps to prepare a future workforce plays a key role. Career academies require a central focus and creative scheduling, and not all states and districts have adopted the career academy model. However, this type of partner is fully engaged in the educational process and highly valued. See www.ncacinc.com with the National Career Academy Coalition for more information on career academies.

Certainly, career academy partners, with their active engagement in the educational process, serve as a positive marketing tool for the school and administration. Business professionals who participate in career academies spread the word about the quality of education students are receiving and how a principal supports the business community. This type of support is unequivocal and far-reaching. The district, school administration, and students all benefit from an academy partnership, especially the students. See figure 6.2 for a sample academy partnership contract.

Many businesses may question how they can support such a large financial commitment. Truly, it is not difficult. Imagine that a CEO or VP of a company, who is estimated to make $200 per hour, teaches a class of thirty students for an hour. Because time is valuable, time is included in the support.

> **Academy Partnership Agreement**
>
> This Academy Partnership Agreement is between the (District) and the (Business/Organization.
>
> **I. Factual Background**
>
> Whereas, the district desires to build strong community support of and involvement in its Academy of (fill in the blank) at (school name);
>
> Whereas, the district desires to provide its students and teachers in the Academy of (fill in the blank) at (school name) with a greater practical understanding of the (defined area of academy).
>
> Whereas, the (business/organization) desires to support its community and assist students in obtaining practical knowledge and skills related to the (name field).
>
> Now therefore, the district and (business/organization), in consideration of the mutual promises set forth in this Agreement, the receipt and sufficiency of which are hereby acknowledged, agree as follows:
>
> **II. Term**
>
> This Agreement if for the term of (X) years, commencing on (date) and ending on (date).
>
> **III. Business/Organization Duties and Responsibilities**
>
> Donations
> The (business/organization) shall make equipment and in-kind donations to "X" Academy at (school). The donations to the "X" Academy must have a total value of at least $100,000 for the first year of the Agreement and $25,000 of total value for the next three years of this agreement.
>
> The (business/organization) shall submit a list of proposed values of materials and equipment purchased for the "X" Academy. In-kind donations will also be included with proposed values.
>
> The (business/organization) shall submit a log of time spent with the teachers and students of the "X" Academy. Each hour spent equated to a dollar amount that shall be included in the total value of the agreement. Time is equated as follows:
>
> Hourly rate of employee x time spent x number of contacts = Value
>
> **IV. Naming Rights**
>
> The District shall provide the (business/industry) exclusive naming rights for the "X" Academy.
>
> **V. Branding**
>
> The District shall enter into a branding agreement with (business/organization) and the academy shall be named the "X" Academy.
> Specific branding and advertising shall be agreed upon and may include:
> 1. Displaying the business logo within the Academy.
> 2. Displaying on school website.
> 3. Displaying in school newsletter.
> 4. Providing link to (business/organization) on school web page.
> 5. Press release.
> 6. Academy certificate.
> 7. Public displays of (business/organization) in and around school.
> 8. Other marketing strategies agreed upon.
>
> **VI. Annual Meeting**
> The District and the (business/organization) shall meet twice annually to determine the status and progress of the academy partnership. Parties may recommend alterations to agreement, if needed.

Figure 6.2   Sample Academy Partnership Contract.

Thirty students have to be calculated at an hour per student. So, the calculation is as follows:

$$\$200/\text{hr} \times 30 \text{ students} = \$6{,}000 \text{ investment}$$

Now, imagine the business supporting a teacher externship, wherein the teachers in the academy visit the worksite for three hours to learn about market demands. The calculation would depend on the rate of pay of the business individual who coordinates the visit.

$$\$25/hr \times 8 \text{ teachers} \times 3 \text{ hours} = \$600 \text{ investment}$$

Through using this method, the financial investment can add up quickly. More time and talent is needed, rather than funds. This type of partnership adds value, relevance, and importance to what the students are learning and how the teachers teach the material. Business appreciates the public acknowledgment of the investment, and students are more motivated to become college and career ready.

CHEERLEADING

The principal should, in effect, be the head cheerleader for a school. When the principal is seen advocating for and celebrating students and teachers, in all of their endeavors, a culture of celebration and expectation is developed. Kathleen Trail (2000) pointed out that principals should praise, praise, praise teacher accomplishments and success in the effort to create school reform. The same is true for student programs and accomplishments. Simply put, singing the praises and accomplishments of students and staff builds support in the school and the school community.

Administrators need to make this praise a regular routine in multiple outlets. In doing so, a culture of excellence is being built and expected. The self-fulfilling prophecy, again, is real.

If the principal wants to grow a program, the principal needs only to praise the program and personally market the program with students. Participation in the program will increase because students look to the principal for the lead, just as the community does. The principal needs to understand that he/she is responsible for the school brand. How does the principal want the community and the students who attend the school to view the school? Marketing the message continually builds the brand of excellence.

Marketing tools are often overlooked at the principal level, maybe due to non-familiarity with those said tools. However, a principal should build a marketing plan for the school. This plan should include elements such as the school's website, the use of social media such as Facebook and/or Twitter, a principal's blog, principal newsletters, local newsprint, community events, and so on. The message should be on point and consistent, whatever that message is.

Repeating the same message in every avenue brands the school. For example, the principal may develop his/her own hashtag—"#(name of school)

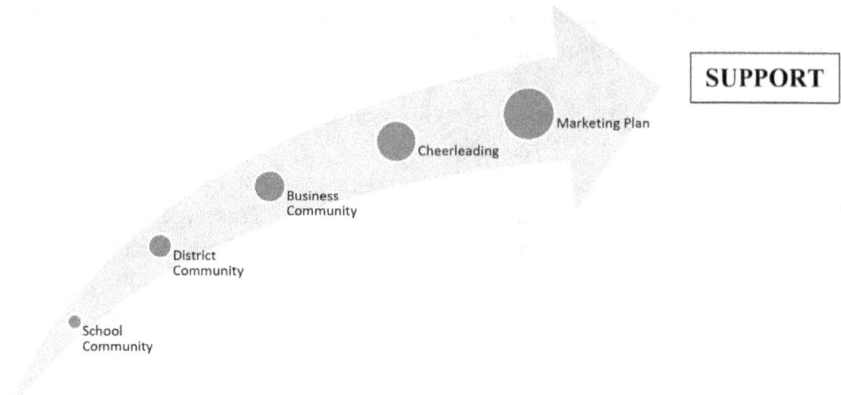

Figure 6.3   Elements of a Support System.

nation." After discussing or posting about a success or event, the hashtag is repeated over and over. Luke Summerfield (2014), stated:

> One of the most powerful things you can do is to create a branded term to refer to all your employees and customers. Link it back to the core idea of your brand and promote the idea as they are a part of some exclusive "tribe." Create a special celebration process to praise them for joining your tribe and get them excited for being a part of something bigger than themselves (para 6).

In essence, the principal creates a culture where students, parents, teachers, and the business community are excited to be a part of that culture. To maintain the excitement, the principal should continually employ marketing strategies and be the biggest cheerleader for the school.

Systems Perspective

In order to develop a system's perspective on building a culture of support, principals need to review all elements and develop a plan of attack. See figure 6.3 for elements of a support system. Each element must be strategically planned in order to garner the maximum support. Determining timelines, processes and procedures, and persons responsible for each component is critical to success. Just as the principal schedules visibility with school events, this type of support system should be scheduled as well.

PROGRESS MONITORING

In table 6.2, the beginning of a sample strategic support plan is provided to demonstrate the development of a support system. Notice that the table

Table 6.2 Sample Beginning of a Support Plan

Strategy	Who?	What?	When?	How?	Evaluated?
Community Needs Assessment	Administration, Guidance	Determine the needs and issues facing the community	Beginning of the year	Surveys to staff, civic organizations, and churches	Data analysis to determine areas of focus, share with leadership team to identify goals
Community Service Focus	Leadership Team, staff sponsors of student groups	Build-in community service projects to focus on identified community needs	All year–each group should provide a calendar of events/activities	Written plan created with students	Evidence of service activity with log of time spent and any impact made
Civic Organization Membership	Principal	Principal joins local civic organization to engage with the community leaders and share news of school	Weekly meetings	Block time and share results with faculty	Benefits of membership are tracked through partnerships, survey of attitudes of school from civic group
Visibility	Administration	Coverage of school events	All year	Develop a calendar of events for each month and denote coverage	Survey of parents and students

includes the basic information as well as how the strategy will be evaluated. This progress monitoring is important as a principal wants to ensure that the efforts are creating the desired effect—support for the school.

Surveys should be created in advance of any initiative that plans to use a survey for progress monitoring, as well as any logs or any other tracking system. Sharing these tools in advance with the intended audiences lets them know what you are hoping to attain through the partnerships and engagement. In doing so, transparency is evident, which, in turn, helps to build trust. Of course, the plan below is just a beginning. Each part discussed in this chapter should be included.

SUMMARY

In order for principals to garner the support they need, principals must show support for the school and the community. The first way to do this is to be present. This presence extends to not only the hallways and classrooms of the school but also to athletic events, club meetings, competitions, and community service events. An administrator's presence opens the door for engagement, which is essential to build trust. Scheduling visibility can be tricky, but it is necessary to ensure equal access to all student groups.

Actively participating in booster clubs and civic organizations is another way to build community, and thus support. These organizations want an administrator to be involved, as it shows interest in their children and ease of communication. Principals need to be approachable, and sometimes community members need an avenue to approach. Administrators must also remember their district community and the challenges they face. Therefore, it is important to credit a district community with the support of the school's successes. In doing this, administrators are more likely to continue to receive support!

Business partners and academy partners are important relationships that need to be recruited, cultivated, and sustained. A business partner's support is much different than an academy partner's support, but all community support is welcome. Allowing for partnership contracts explicitly spells out the benefits of the relationship to both parties. These partnerships should be evaluated annually.

The principal should be the biggest cheerleader for a school, taking every opportunity to sing the praises of the students, the staff, and the community. When the principal talks, the community listens; a positive message can be infectious.

A PIECE-AT-A-TIME

- How can a school help alleviate community issues?
- What is an easy way principals can open lines of communication and help build community trust?
- How can a school help build district support?
- What is the difference between a business partner and academy partner?
- What is the best way a principal ensures continued business support?
- What is the value of joining a local civic organization?
- How can the principal become the head cheerleader of a school?
- How does a school administration employ marketing principles?
- How does a principal build a system of support?

REFERENCES

Adams, C. M., & Forsyth, P. B. (2007). Promoting a culture of parent collaboration and trust: An empirical study. *Journal of School Public Relations, 28*(1), 32–56.

Boyd, Alesha Williams, & Michelle Gladden. More Students Turn to Career Academies. *USA Today*, May 27, 2013, www.usatoday.com/story/money/business/2013/05/27/career-academies-find-seat-in-schools/2364421/.

Bryk, A. & Schneider, B. (2003) Trust in schools: A core resource for school reform. *Educational Leadership, 60*(6), 40–45.

Dinham, S. (2005). Principal leadership for outstanding educational outcomes. *Journal of Educational Administration, 43*(4), 338–356.

Every Student Succeeds Act (2015 - S. 1177). *GovTrack.us*, www.govtrack.us/congress/bills/114/s1177.

Fritch, W. (1999). An overlooked role of high school athletics: The formation of social capital through parent involvement. Paper presented at the *Annual Meeting of the American Educational Research Association*, Montreal, QC.

Green, T. L. & Gooden, M. A. (2014). Transforming out-of-school challenges into opportunities: Community schools reform in the urban midwest. *Urban Education, 49*(8), 930–954.

Khalifa, M. (2012). A Re-New-Ed paradigm in successful urban school leadership: Principal as community leader. *Educational Administration Quarterly, 48*(3), 424–467.

Lionsclub.org – Lions Club Resources and Information. (n.d.). Retrieved from http://www.lionsclub.org/

National Career Academy Coalition (2018). *NCAC Past, Present and Future*. Retrieved from https://www.ncacinc.com/about/history

Rotary Mottoes (n.d.). Retrieved from https://www.rotary.org/en/rotary-mottoes.

Simon, B. & Epstein, J. (2001). School, family and community partnerships: Linking theory to practice. In: Hiat-Michael, D. (Ed.), *Promising Practice for Family Involvement in Schools* (pp. 1–24). Greenwich, CT: IAP.

Summerfield, L. (2014). How to build a brand that attracts die-hard followers. *Entrepreneur* (April). Retrieved from https://www.entrepreneur.com/article/232805.

Trail, K. (2000). Taking the lead: The role of the principal in school reform. *CSRD Connections, 1*(4), 2–9.

Chapter 7

School and Community Communications

The single biggest problem in communication is the illusion that it has taken place.

—*George Bernard Shaw*

The final chapter is based on communications because communications help to build relationships—either positive or negative. The hope is that in building a comprehensive communication system within the school and within the community, all stakeholders share the same vision and can sing the same tune. Without strong communications, the message is often lost or muddled. In the absence of quality communication, the message that is heard is anyone's guess. School culture is highly dependent upon and influenced by the quality and quantity of communications (Stellar, 2009).

COMMUNICATION WITHIN A SCHOOL

Announcements

One of the first avenues administrators used to convey information in a school is through announcements. Announcements over an intercom system, however, are often unheard and ineffective. Announcements are normally given during a homeroom period or when classes are just beginning or ending. Imagine students either settling into a class, still talking with their friends, while they get class materials together. Teachers are also trying to get class organized for instruction. Worse yet, imagine students packing up all materials with the excitement of going home for the day.

Intercom announcements are not always the best method of communication; however, they are necessary at times. Honestly, daily intercom announcements only work if the routine is set with all teachers and students that all students are seated and paying attention at a predetermined time of day. McNamara and Murphy (2008) recognized that routines for children inform their practices. Therefore, the regularly determined interval will reduce the noise of transition, thus allowing for communications to be received.

Additionally, teachers resent frequent announcements that may interfere with instructional time. Teachers are already pressured to teach too many standards in a short period of time; therefore, interferences with announcements should be minimal and meaningful. Scheduling announcements strategically at the beginning of the day and at the end of the day is sufficient. The smart practitioner will build the time in the bell schedule for announcements, preventing a reduction in instructional time.

Schools that have media announcements, meaning announcements that are conveyed through a media system such as televisions or SMART boards are more effective. Then, students and teachers can not only hear but can also see the administrator. The entertainment value is higher, and students today are used to begin entertained. Additionally, when administrators elect to have students assist with announcements, students are more apt to pay attention, because they relate to their peers.

Emails

Emails, like announcements, that address the entire faculty can be a useful tool for communicating within a school; however, emails should also be kept to a minimum. Principals often complain about the sheer number of emails they have to respond to each day as do teachers. In a 2018 study on the effects of email on burnout, the results showed that it was not the volume of email that predicted burnout, but it was the perception of the volume of email requiring attention and response that contributed to burnout (Estévez-Mujica & Quintane, 2018).

With that being said, principals need to establish an email routine so teachers do not feel bombarded by administrative emails. An email routine could include weekly announcements, bus schedules, and school events. The marketing rule entitled the "Rule of 7" was discovered in the 1930s by big movie executives, and this rule stated that an audience needs to hear a message at least seven times for it to be remembered (Kruse, 2018). Applying that logic to school communications, emails play an important role. A sample email schedule could look like table 7.1. Coupled with announcements and other avenues, the Rule of 7 can be obeyed.

Table 7.1 Sample Email Schedule

Time	Monday	Tuesday	Wednesday	Thursday	Friday
7:30 a.m.	Monday Update—Outlines all events and meetings for the week				
9:00 a.m.	Attendance email listing those students out for disciplinary reasons	Attendance email listing those students out for disciplinary reasons	Attendance email listing those students out for disciplinary reasons	Attendance email listing those students out for disciplinary reasons	Attendance email listing those students out for disciplinary reasons
2:45 p.m.	Afternoon announcement email for teachers to share with students (late buses, events for next day).	Afternoon announcement email for teachers to share with students (late buses, events for next day).	Afternoon announcement email for teachers to share with students (late buses, events for next day).	Afternoon announcement email for teachers to share with students (late buses, events for next day).	Afternoon announcement email for teachers to share with students (late buses, events for next day).

Of course, adding announcements to this schedule increases the reinforcement opportunities for teachers and students. As noticed in table 7.1, teachers are reading announcements to students as well as students hearing the announcements twice a day. See table 7.2 for a sample schedule for emails and announcements.

By adhering to this type of schedule, students and teachers know when information is coming and when it should be shared. This allows for that important routine to be established for all parties. When communications are haphazard, critical information can be missed. This is not to say that these are the only times emails and announcements are made; however, this schedule allows teachers and students to have an expectation of communication. That expectation provides consistency that helps to convey a positive message.

The above example references a Monday Update email. This email should be concise and consistent, as stated above. In this email, administrators are given a prime opportunity to not only reinforce the communication of school events but also recognize and provide positive feedback to teachers. In doing so, teachers are more apt to pay attention to the emails. See figure 7.1 for example.

Call-Out Systems

Many school districts have purchased a call-out system that allows schools to place automatic phone calls to parents when a student is absent. These same systems allow schools to automatically place phone calls to parents about school events or in the case of emergency. These systems can be very beneficial to schools and parents. However, administrators make mistakes when the system is overused.

Just like with school announcements and emails, school call-out announcements should be on a schedule that is not cumbersome. Parents need to be informed of this schedule (day and time) in advance so they know when to expect the phone call. If schools overuse this system, parents will not answer the phone calls or not listen to them intently. In fact, this system needs to be used sparingly. Aside from the attendance phone calls and emergencies, schools need to limit these calls to once a week, if possible.

A good idea is to schedule this phone call on Monday nights to outline the events of the week; however, these phone call needs to be short. This may take some practice to get it right, but phone calls that are too long are tuned out as well. Coinciding this phone call with the Monday Update email/announcement allows students and parents to discuss the school events together. Parents need advance notice and to hear the same message multiple times, just like teachers and students. Discussion of other avenues of communication will follow.

Table 7.2 Sample Email/Announcement Schedule

Time	Mode	Monday	Tuesday	Wednesday	Thursday	Friday
7:30	Email	Monday Update email—outlines all teacher and student events and meetings for the week. Teachers share school events.				
7:45	Announcement	School events, character education	School events, character education	School events, character education	School events, character education	School events, character education
9:00	Email	Attendance email listing those students out for disciplinary reasons	Attendance email listing those students out for disciplinary reasons	Attendance email listing those students out for disciplinary reasons	Attendance email listing those students out for disciplinary reasons	Attendance email listing those students out for disciplinary reasons
2:45	Email	Afternoon announcement email for teachers to share with students (late buses, events for next day).	Afternoon announcement email for teachers to share with students (late buses, events for next day).	Afternoon announcement email for teachers to share with students (late buses, events for next day).	Afternoon announcement email for teachers to share with students (late buses, events for next day).	Afternoon announcement email for teachers to share with students (late buses, events for next day).
2:55	Announcement	Afternoon announcement—reminder of daily events and bus information	Afternoon announcement—reminder of daily events and bus information	Afternoon announcement—reminder of daily events and bus information	Afternoon announcement—reminder of daily events and bus information	Afternoon announcement—reminder of daily events and bus information

To: XYZ Staff
FR: Principal
DATE: Monday, Oct. 12, 2020

Good morning XYZ Fighting Tigers! Please see below for the week's events.

Monday
4:00   Faculty Meeting in Auditorium
7:00   Varsity Volleyball at home

Tuesday
ALL DAY – Required Embedded PD *Constructing Quality Assessments* in MC Classroom
5:00 Girls Tennis at home
4:30 Boys Tennis away at THS

Wednesday
ALL DAY – PLC's using Planning Protocol
4:30 Cross Country at State County Park

Thursday
6:00 JV Football away at CHS

Friday
2:30 Pep Rally in Gym
7:30 Varsity Football at home

Weekly Kudos:
Mr. Johnson - helping the after school tutoring program
Mrs. Leslie – taking the lead on the winter coat drive
Mrs. Saul – taking the lead on the can food drive
Mrs. Whitaker – covering a class for a sick colleague
Mr. Tony – helping build drama set
Ms. Smith – sponsoring the new Book Club

Figure 7.1   Sample Monday Update Email.

Halls and Walls

Do not underestimate the value of marketing of events and messages in your school by using the physical space. One of the first rules of marketing is location, and the second rule of marketing is to see rule number 1 (Blanton, 2000). Well, the same is true for schools. The entrances where students and parents first enter the building as well as the front office are considered prime spaces. Your school's vision and mission should be prominent along with pertinent information on upcoming events.

The front office space should not be cluttered but should be welcoming with announcements displayed so that visitors are first drawn to those announcements and important messages. An electronic display with important announcements for the week as well as positive praises should be included in this space. In essence, the front office is the first place parents and visitors enter a school for any length of time. Make use of the captured audience and communicate with your audience.

Within the school, major gathering areas such as a common area, cafeteria, media center, and entrance to a gym are also important marketing spaces that are often underutilized. Students and the community want to have a sense of pride in their schools, so provide them with the right message in these spaces. Give them something to talk about, but make sure the message is the one you want conveyed. Club meetings, awards, and recognitions, important school events, and the like should all be displayed as many times as possible in the school.

Within the classroom, the same truth holds apparent. If teachers are displaying the events of the school and making sure that students are aware of events for the week or month, students are more apt to receive the message. Imagine walking through the doors of a school and seeing the message, sitting in the common areas and seeing the message, and seeing the message in the classroom along with the other avenues of communication already discussed, students have experienced multiple reinforcements of the same message thus far. Not only have the students received the message but so have the teachers and parents.

MEETINGS

Schools undoubtedly hold a plethora of meetings. However, developing a systemic way to convey the vision of the school at every meeting, whether it is a faculty meeting or a professional development meeting is important. This message gives the teachers the "why" of what they do. Regular reporting progress is important during these meetings as well, so that teachers feel a sense of ownership in the achievements of a school. The same is true for parents.

During Parent-Teacher Association (PTA) meetings or booster club meetings, parents need to hear how the school is performing in achieving its mission. The repetition of the mission statement (the why) and the plan to achieve along with the progress of that achievement (the how) keeps parents engaged. They want to know what is happening in their school to help their children. Therefore, taking advantage of every opportunity with an audience is crucial to communicating the message that schools care and are working hard for the children they serve.

These meetings are also a good place to announce important upcoming events. Parents do not always get the phone calls that are sent weekly. Often, emails are skipped due to time constraints. Therefore, announcing events and successes at all meetings possible allows for another avenue of reinforcement. The same is true for teachers. Teachers get so busy during the day that announcements of upcoming events can be forgotten. Remind them during every meeting possible. The more they hear and see it, the more they will remember it.

Unfortunately, parent involvement/engagement decreases as children progress from elementary school to high school (Green & Walker, 2007). Remember that elementary PTA meeting, that is, standing room only versus the high-school PTA meeting with only fifteen parents in attendance. This problem is not uncommon. Even though older children often express that they are fine without their parents in attendance of events, the attendance and participation matters.

Parents also often express that they are not invited to engage in the upper grades with their children. However, the more a parent is engaged in their child's school, student achievement increases (Ho & Willms, 1996; Redding, Langdon, Meyer & Sheley, 2004). Therefore, every opportunity to invite parents to participate in events, even as a spectator, is important. Informing parents of the progress of the school's vision and how they can help their children succeed is also critical to engagement. Sometimes, the parent only needs an invitation.

Leadership teams and department chairs are a great way to convey messages in a school. These anchor teachers are teachers that help to set the tone and shape the culture of the school. Teachers look to the anchor teachers for their reactions and engagement. These anchor teachers can help to spread the word of events, meetings, successes, and needed focus in the school. Administrators need to make sure that their anchor teachers are helping to reinforce the message in schools, and this can be done by providing a template for the meetings. See figure 7.2 for an example agenda for a department meeting.

With this type of agenda, administrators can ensure that meetings are focused on the work of schools. Without a focus for the meetings, these meetings can quickly evolve into a session of complaints: peer interactions, student behaviors, etc. With a focus, however, teachers enter the meeting with a goal, and the needed work can be done in a much more effective and efficient manner. Additionally, the conditions are right for teachers to hear the message: celebration of success as well as areas of focus as they tie to the school's mission. Announcements added during these meetings serve as a reminder and provide an avenue for engagement.

XYZ School
English Department Meeting
October 21, 2020
Mission: To Ensure All Students Succeed.

I. Literacy Celebrations
   a. October Progress Monitoring Results
   b. Media Center circulation numbers
II. Data Analysis
   a. Standards of growth
   b. Plans for standards of focus
   c. Proficiency Rates
III. Curriculum
   a. Next Units
   b. Material Needs
IV. Reflection
   a. How did we make sure all students are succeeding?
   b. How did we respond when students did not succeed?
   c. What needs do you have?
V. Parent Communications
   a. Parent Logs
   b. Concerns
VI. Announcements
   a. Homecoming Week
      i. Float assignments
      ii. Pep Rally Volunteers
      iii. Parent Communications
   b. Embedded PD
   c. School Improvement Council Meeting

Figure 7.2   Sample Department Meeting Agenda.

COMMUNITY COMMUNICATIONS

Marquee

A school's marquee is an effective way to communicate an important message to the entire community and helps to get your school noticed (Pawlas, 2005). This marquee should be updated frequently so that it does not lose its impact. If a marquee remains unchanged for weeks, people will tend to stop looking. Therefore, an administrator needs to have a system for regular updates of the marquee. Parents and students need to know when the updates will occur as well, which helps to focus their attention.

Including the personnel responsible for the updates in developing the plan is important so that expectations are clear. For example, updating the marquee every Monday and Thursday mornings could be a reasonable expectation. This will allow for events to be listed as well as highlights awards or successes. With the advent of electronic marquees, this type of communication is much easier. However, do not underestimate the power of the written word on a marquee. Be sure that communication is clear, correct, and concise.

Newsletters

School newsletters are an excellent way to communicate school news and progress. In the health industry, it has been found that newsletters are generally read and actually impact health practices (Kalba, 1973; Waterson et al., 2009). Why would this medium not transfer to education? It does. Administrators should regularly produce newsletters to inform parents and students about the school to include events, progress made toward the school's mission, plans, programs, and awards and recognitions.

The schedule for the newsletter needs to be made in advance and communicated with parents so they know to expect it. In fact, the date of the newsletter should be advertised in the call out, the email system, and the marquee. The newsletter should not be too long, so as not to lose parents' interest. However, a newsletter can be filled with student and teacher successes as well as upcoming events. Again, school pride is built and becomes part of the culture.

Additionally, a newsletter that goes to the entire school community is a great place to recognize those businesses that support a school. Businesses love the recognition, as the advertisement helps to build a customer base and customer loyalty. Parents love to see the recognition because they feel that businesses are invested in their children's success. In essence, the message that is sent is that the school is a central part of the community.

Newsletters can also become a project for the school itself. If teachers want to submit for publication in the newsletter, that is a great way for them to toot their own horns. A system of submissions needs to be in place. See figure 7.3 for a sample submission form. The same is true for any student group or organization. In fact, a class in the school can help to create the newsletter for the administration, as long as the administrator has final editing rights. In this instance, the principal may have a "Principal's Corner" to relay timely messages as a part of the newsletter. Consider a newsletter going home every month as a good rule of time.

XYZ School
Newsletter Submission Request

Name_____   Date_____

Topic: _____

Text:

You can enter text here or attach a Word Document of no more than 200 words.

_____
_____
_____
_____
_____
_____
_____
_____
_____
_____

Do you have pictures? _____ YES   _____ NO

If yes, please attach.

You can send this form electronically to the principal's secretary by the end of the 3rd week of the month or you can print and submit in person.

Figure 7.3   Sample Newsletter Submission Form.

News Media Outlets

Administrators should know their district's policy on media releases. Normally, the policy does not prevent administrators from submitting positive press about their schools but serves to manage unwanted media attention. Therefore, administrators should have a developed media contact list for all local news sources. These sources should include print and news. Establishing good relationships with the media only serves to promote the school in a positive light.

Not only is it important to have the right contacts for each media outlet, but principals should know their submission dates. For example, a local paper may require an article to be submitted a week or two before publication. Each outlet's deadlines may vary, so having a contact sheet with deadlines is important. If individuals in the school are charged with this type of promotion, then a reporting system needs to be developed so that the principal is fully aware of every notice to the media. See figure 7.4 for a sample media reporting form.

A good rule of thumb is to try to submit something to a media outlet once a week. Not all articles will be picked up, of course. However, your odds of positive press increase dramatically with this type of practice. What a way for the community to see the good works and rally behind a school! Even local news media like to be given advance notice of any special programs or events happing at a school. On slow news days, these news packages make for great press. When the majority of the news heard on television is negative, positive stories tend to stand out.

Managing all of the positive press can be cumbersome. That is why the attention needed for this part of building school culture is often inadequate. Does the principal have to do it all? The answer is no, of course. However, the principal needs to have a system in place to manage it all. Principals should never, if possible, be unaware of media attention, never. Therefore, examining the existing school structure to determine what avenues best help fulfill the need is essential.

The first step is to examine the existing courses that support media releases. Does the school have a journalism class that can assist? Can the school's student council representative group take a lead? What about leadership classes or service-learning classes? All of these courses have teachers who act as the responsible adult overseeing the projects. Writing media releases can become part of the weekly work that is shared. The next step is to assign an administrator to progress monitor the work of these classes to ensure that releases are being submitted by the required deadlines. Is this enough?

Date	Name	Submission Title	Topic	Media Outlet

Figure 7.4 Sample Media Reporting Form.

No, all media releases should be proofed by the principal. As stated earlier, media attention should not be a surprise to the principal of a school. The principal is the one responsible, and lack of awareness is no excuse for poorly written releases. Every newsletter, parent email, call-out, marquee announcement, and media release reflects on the district, the school, and the administration. Therefore, a system of checks and balances needs to be in place to ensure quality is conveyed.

Churches or Social Gathering Places

Administrators should never underestimate the value of communication with local churches. Church families tend to have great influence over the beliefs of its members. Local ministers, pastors, preachers, etc. therefore, have great influence in the communities they serve. Consequently, it is smart for administrators to keep this in mind when communicating a message. Visiting the churches that your community attends is a great place to start, but that is not enough.

Those newsletters, discussed in a previous section, share them with the churches. Once a month, the newsletters can be shared and highlighted in church bulletins. By allowing the families to celebrate successes together, community spirit is built-in support of the school. In addition to the newsletters, your weekly call-outs and emails can go to the heads of the churches as well, if they agree, of course. In doing so, the announcements are shared in the home and the church. Again, repetition is important.

In areas that are rural, minority, and/or poverty stricken, the importance of the local churches cannot be overstated. Taylor and Chatters (1988) found that the church is a fundamental source of social support for the African American Community, and this should be no surprise. In addition, Billingsley and Caldwell (1991) stated that the school is a highly valued and revered institution as African American parents want their children to be successful; they value success for their children, as most do. As values may be consistent, beliefs may not.

Beliefs are shaped by experiences, and school administrators need to give parents a different experience. This experience comes in the form of communicating with them where they meet instead of expecting parents to come to you. If your school has a plan to increase student achievement results, ask to speak in the local churches and share that plan. Inform parents what they can expect and how they can help support the school and their children. After all, children deserve our best, comprehensive efforts.

The same is true if students are to be celebrated. Visit the church and ask to make an announcement to highlight the achievements of the church youth.

Celebrate with them. In doing so, administrators break down communication barriers that may exist due to previous experiences and/or lack of trust. In building this trust, actions speak louder than words. The combination of the two is powerful in building support (Russel, 2016).

Communities also have other meeting places, such as community centers. The same rules apply to these community centers as to churches. Administrators have to take the communication to the people. This responsibility certainly can be shared with the administrative team. The same is true with civic groups, such as the local Rotary Club, Lions Club, or Exchange Club. Again, communicating with the community in their gathering places has a bigger impact and can prevent miscommunication, the antithesis to a positive culture.

Social Media

Social media are generally referred to as internet-based channels of mass personal communication, and social media's influence in society is undeniable. In 2015, 65 percent of adults were found to use social media networking sites, an increase from 7 percent over a ten-year time span (Perrin, 2015). Additionally, a large number of parents of school-age children belong to Gen Y (age group 25–39), and this generation finds social media as a vehicle for engagement (Naim & Lenka, 2017). The education system's challenge is to find effective ways to use social media to its advantage without disrupting instruction.

The use of social media as a communication tool can be most powerful. In fact, all levels of educational systems have begun to embrace using social media to communicate with its stakeholders (Wang, 2013). With the use of multiple social media sites, the same message can be communicated to varying groups. For example, Facebook usage as a social media vehicle is most utilized by the age groups that span the ages of 18–49 (Chen, 2020). So, this media tool has a broad scope, whereas Instagram is most notably used by the span of ages 18–24 (Chen, 2020). See table 7.3 for demographic data on most utilized social media sites (Chen, 2020).

Of course, there are other social media sites like SnapChat and LinkedIn that continue to be developed. However, Facebook, Instagram, and Twitter are the most universal sites visited. What this should tell educators is that it is

Table 7.3 Social Media Usage Percentages (Chen, 2020)

Site	Age 18–24 (%)	Age 25–30 (%)	Age 30–49 (%)	Age 50–64 (%)
Facebook	76	84	79	68
Instagram	75	57	47	23
Twitter	44	31	26	17

time to fully utilize these social media networks to communicate a school's message to all stakeholders—students, parents, and the business community. In order to facilitate communication with all age groups and stakeholders, the best policy is to use the most utilized sights.

Developing a system of managing these sights is critical because posts reach so many of the intended audience. Messages of academic achievements, upcoming events, sporting accomplishments, and community support help to build a culture of pride that has been so often mentioned. Students who graduate from a school system continue to follow their alma maters on these sights, and the pride continues to grow.

Does the principal need to be the singular person managing and posting on all sites? This is not necessarily the case; however, the principal does need to monitor all of the sites and have access to delete and modify posts. This is to say, that the principal should have the final editing power simply, because the principal is the one who will answer for the posts in the eyes of the district and the community.

Posts should be consistently updated in order to keep the audience's attention. In addition, questions asked by the stakeholders on these sights should be answered. Just as social media can provide a positive avenue of communication, the opposite can be true. Principals need to be vigilant in conveying the right message in a timely fashion and consistently. Careful consideration of word choice, grammar, and picture selection should be given.

Today, many neighborhoods, clubs, and organizations utilize their own special groups within these networks. Members of these groups have to be approved to see the group's postings. In these groups, stakeholders often speak their minds, and it is not always positive. It is important to know what is being said, even if those concerns are not always specifically addressed. However, concerns that should be addressed can be addressed in a timely fashion. Therefore, it is a good idea to have someone or know someone who is a member of these groups who will inform administrators of any community issue.

When using these sights, it is a good practice to repeat the school's mission or slogan. Remember, repetition breads remembrance. A great marketing tool is the use of a hashtag (#), as mentioned in a previous chapter. For example, the principal may use #SchoolXYZFightingTigers! In utilizing this hashtag over and over, administrators should encourage parents and students who post on social media to use the same hashtag. The use of the hashtag allows for all posts and tweets to be easily searched, viewed, and supported.

What this means is that if a parent posted a picture of his child throwing a football and posted "#SchoolXYZFightingTigers!" along with the picture, that picture can be found by all stakeholders. Publicizing this hashtag allows school spirit to grow. In fact, all social media identification should be advertised to all stakeholders, so they can follow the information flowing from the school. These social media handles should be a part of every newsletter and email sent to the school community as well.

Remember, these social media sites should be updated regularly with new postings several times a week. This keeps the information relevant and fresh, ensuring that stakeholders continue to engage. Parents and students love to see pictures of celebrations, success and hard work. They love to share those pictures and spread the pride. However, there is a catch with the pictures selected. Principals need to make sure that no pictures are posted of students whose parents do not give permission. Media releases are vital to prevent litigation.

Web Pages

Unlike social media sites that are real time, web pages are designed to contain the most standard information. This permanence can change from year to year, so it is vitally important to keep the school's web page updated. Information about school calendars, programs and clubs, athletic schedules, club meetings and competition schedules, faculty contact information, and the like should all be a part of a school's web page. The guidance portion of a school's web page should include resources to help parents with their children. These resources evolve with the age group associated with the school.

For example, an elementary school may have parenting tips as part of the guidance page, whereas a high school may have information on college applications, student financial aid, and scholarship information. Athletic programs should include all athletic schedules. It is helpful to include club meeting schedules as well because too often, parents and students complain that they don't know when certain clubs meet.

In addition to guidance programs and athletic programs, information that should always be included are the principal's communications. This category of information should include the monthly newsletters that are distributed as well as the school renewal plan. With the school renewal plan, it is helpful for the principal to attach a word document explaining the goals and strategies used to achieve the goals. The school renewal plan should be well known by all stakeholders in order to facilitate ownership.

The web page should be updated each summer to correct for changes in schedules as well as changes in faculty. Nothing is more frustrating than to go on a school's web page and not be able to find what you are looking for. So, administrators need to regularly check the web page during the school year for needed updates and accuracy of information as well as ease of access to information. Because the web page contains so much information, it is helpful to break the different components down to make the updating more manageable. The web page should also provide the links to the social media accounts.

SYSTEMS APPROACH

In order to develop a strong communication system, each component part needs to be discussed with the school's leadership along with the expectations for each. Then, the sharing and assigning of responsibilities can begin. However, without the expectations being made clear, the results may not derive the desired effect. See table 7.4 for a sample chart of expectations. Once the "what" and the "who" is determined, the plan need only be executed with regularity and progress monitored.

SUMMARY

School and community communications are integral to building a positive school culture. These communications should be comprehensive and well planned in order to get the desired effect. If not, the lack of communication speaks volumes to the stakeholders, and this is not the culture that administrators desire. Additionally, plans to reinforce and repeat the communications should be included, as people need to hear the same message at least seven times for it to stick.

A school communication plan should include a concise use of announcements and emails. Too many announcements interrupt class instruction. However, well-timed announcements that are expected and allowed for in the bell schedule can convey important information if the expectation is clear in the classrooms. Emails should also be concise and on a schedule, if at all possible. This advertised schedule helps to reinforce the expectation of actually reading the emails.

Like announcements and emails, the school's use of a call-out system should be scheduled and concise. Parents and students need to know when call-outs are scheduled so that they will be sure to listen. Otherwise, too many call-outs result in stakeholders not answering the phone or hanging up too soon.

Department and leadership meetings are great avenues to support the mission of the school and ensure that teachers know what is expected as well as the announcements for the school. A template provided for the meetings

Table 7.4 Sample Chart of Communications Expectations

Mode	Expectation	Progress Monitor	Name
Web Page	Updated each summer and once a quarter for additions and checks for accuracy	Web Page Check List of required information checked once a quarter	
Principal Communications	Updated monthly with newsletters, updated yearly with School Renewal Plan	Checked each month	
Guidance	All guidance pages updated monthly	Checked each month for accuracy and timeliness	
Health Services	All policies, screenings, calendars, etc. updated once a year	Checked in the summer	
Faculty Contacts	Updated in the summer and as new hires are added, check all links to ensure they are active and the right people are in the right departments	Checked for accuracy in August and again in December	
Clubs and Activities	Lists with sponsors and meeting times	Updated monthly and checked for accuracy	
Athletics	All athletic programs schedules updated, coaching contacts, policies, etc.	Updated each summer and checked each season for accuracy	
PTA	All PTA meetings, agendas, notes along with fundraiser information and financials	Updated monthly	
School Improvement	All SIC agendas, notes, and plans posted monthly	Updated monthly	
Business/Community Partners	All current business partners listed with level of endorsement, information on time and talent donations with pictures	Updated monthly for accuracy and timeliness, check media releases	
Call Out	List of week's events, short and concise	Listen to calls for clarity	
Monday Update Email	List of week's meetings and events as well as Kudos	Check email before sending	
Announcement Emails	Once in the morning for daily events, once in afternoon for bus and event information	Check email before sending	

(Continued)

Table 7.4 Sample Chart of Communications Expectations (*Continued*)

Mode	Expectation	Progress Monitor	Name
Halls and Walls	Post relevant information on school events in high traffic areas; change weekly	Get approval before posting. Be sure to remove in a timely fashion.	
Department/ Leadership Team Meetings	Provide template for all meetings	Meeting notes submitted and reviewed with administration	
Marquee	Announcements posted on Mondays and Thursdays of each week	A notebook will be kept for all information to be posted in the front office.	
Newsletter	Once a month publication to go home to all stakeholders and posted on the web page. This includes the Principal's Corner.	All newsletters must be proofed and approved by the principal.	
Media Submissions	Once a week submission to a media outlet with an article about the school's successes or programs.	A media submission form is used for all submissions. Principal must approve all media.	
Gathering Places	Monthly meetings with local churches or social gatherings to share messages from the school.	All handouts, presentations must be approved by the principal.	
Facebook	Post once a week, minimum.	Monitor posts, check media releases	
Twitter	Post once a week, minimum.	Monitor posts, check media releases	
Instagram	Post once a week, minimum	Monitor posts, check media releases	

ensures that the information is conveyed as well as ensures that the meetings are productive. These templates with their notes should be shared back with the administrative team for review.

The halls and the walls of high traffic areas are good places to advertise events or post important information as well as to celebrate successes.

Make sure these areas are not too cluttered, like the front office. Clutter creates distraction. Administrators also have to make sure the information is updated regularly to ensure relevance. The same is true for a school's marquee.

Principal newsletters are a great way to convey lots of information monthly. Stakeholders need to know when these newsletters are to be distributed so they can ask for them. Otherwise, they might not make it home. Sharing these newsletters with local businesses and churches is also a good idea so that information is spread throughout the community. Actually attending local churches, civic organizational meetings, and other community events is another way to spread the good deeds and plans of a school.

Media outlets should be used regularly, if the school district's policy allows for it. Planning media releases once a week, even if they are not printed or advertised, ensures more positive press for the school. These measures help to build school pride and support. In addition to the use of media outlets, social media should be used regularly to communicate with stakeholders. Messages should be timely and correct, ensuring that all media releases are abided.

Lastly, the school's web page should contain the more stagnant information, but it should be updated regularly. Staff members change and calendars of events like athletic events and club meetings change regularly, so updates are critical. Stakeholders are frustrated when they cannot find the information needed, so ensuring accuracy and ease of access is critical for positive communications.

A PIECE-AT-A-TIME

- Name at least seven areas of communication that should be utilized in schools.
- When using school emails, announcements, and call-outs, what should administrators consider?
- How can department chairs support the school communication?
- How can you use the physical space of a school to communicate with stakeholders?
- Why is it important to go to the stakeholders with the communication? Explain and give an example.
- How can social media and web pages help support school communication plans?
- What are some pitfalls with social media and web pages?
- How can you organize the school's communication plan to help build school culture?

REFERENCES

Billingsley, A. & Caldwell, C. (1991). The church, the family, and the school in the African American community. *The Journal of Negro Education, 60*(3), 427–440.

Blanton, V. (2000). *The 12 rules of marketing: Your only choice is to lead or migrate.* Lincoln, NE: Writers Club Press.

Chen, J. (2020). Social media demographics to inform your brand's strategy in 2020. *Sprout Social.* Retrieved from www.sproutsocial.com/insights/new-social-media-demographics/#FB-demos

Estévez-Mujica, C. P., & Quintane, E. (2018). E-mail communication patterns and job burnout. *PLoS ONE, 13*(3), e0193966. doi: 10.1371/journal.pone.0193966

Green, C. & Walker, J. (2007). Parents' motivations for involvement in children's education: An empirical test of a theoretical model of parental involvement. *Journal of Educational Psychology, 99*(3), 532–544.

Ho, S. C. & Willms, J. D. (1996). Effects of parental involvement on eighth grade achievement. *Sociology of Education, 69*(2), 126–141.

Kalba, K. (1973). Communicable medicine: Cable television and health services. *Socio-Econ Planning, 7,* 611–632.

Kruse, K. (2018). How social media crushes old school marketing. *Kruse Control,* https://www.krusecontrolinc.com/rule-of-7-how-social-media-crushes-old-school-marketing/

McNamara, P. & Murphy, R. (2008). Developing everyday routines. *Physical and Occupational Therapy in Pediatrics, 8*(2), 141–154.

Naim, M. & Lenka, U. (2017). The impact of social media and collaboration on Gen Y employees' engagement. *International Journal of Development Issues, 16*(3), 289–299.

Pawlas, G. (2005). *The administrator's guide to school-community relations* (2nd edition). New York: Taylor & Francis.

Perrin, A. (2015). *Social media usage: 2005-2015.* Pew Research Center: Internet, Science & Tech. Retrieved from www.pewinternet.org/2015/10/08/social-networking-usage-2005-2015/

Redding, S., Langdon, J., Meyer, J. & Sheley, P. (2004). The effects of comprehensive parent engagement on student learning outcomes. Paper presented at *American Educational Research Association*, San Diego, CA.

Russel, N. (2016). 3 fundamental rules of trust. *Psychology Today.* https://www.psychologytoday.com/us/blog/trust-the-new-workplace-currency/201608/3-fundamental-rules-trust

Stellar, A. (2009). Book review. [Review of the book *Effective communication for school administrators: A necessity in an information age,* by Kowalski, Peterson, & Fusarelli]. *Journal of Scholarship and Practice, 5*(4), 55–56.

Taylor, R. & Chatters, L. (1988). Church members as a source of informal social support. *Review of Religious Research, 30,* 432–438.

Wang, Y. (2013). Social media in schools: A treasure trove or hot potato? *Journal of Cases in Educational Leadership, 16*(1), 56–64.

Waterson, T., Welsh, B., Keane, B., Cook, M., Hammal, D., Parker, L., & McConachie, H. (2009). Improving early relationships: A randomized, controlled trial of an age-paced parenting newsletter. *Pediatrics, 123*(1), 241–247.

Conclusion

Change is inevitable. As most people are uncomfortable with change, change is a universal truth everyone must face. As our society changes as well as workplace demands, schools must keep up with the change in order to truly prepare our students for the future. School administrators have to navigate the sea of changes they face from the national scene with changes in legislative agendas, state priorities, and district leadership, not to mention societal changes.

As if that was not enough, administrators have to successfully steer the change in order to prepare students and support teachers in the process. The first book *Putting the Pieces Together: A Systems Approach to School Leadership* in combination with *The Final Piece: A Systems Approach to School Leadership* provides a manual of sorts for administrators. This manual is designed to help administrators develop the systems needed in order to successfully manage the change needed.

Throughout the first book and this book, the construction of a schoolhouse analogy is used to suggest a systems design, with the foundation as the systems lens needed to organize the work of schools. The first two major systems addressed in the first book mirror the construction phases, as each system serves a function that helps to support the other. Remember the four major systems in figure C.1.

The systems lens provides the foundation and the system of curriculum and instruction serves as the framing which yields the function and form. Without a system of curriculum and instruction, schools undermine their purpose. The second system—the vertical support—includes teacher supports. Teacher supports are necessary to support the system of curriculum and instruction. Naturally, these two systems come first and are discussed in the first book.

120   Conclusion

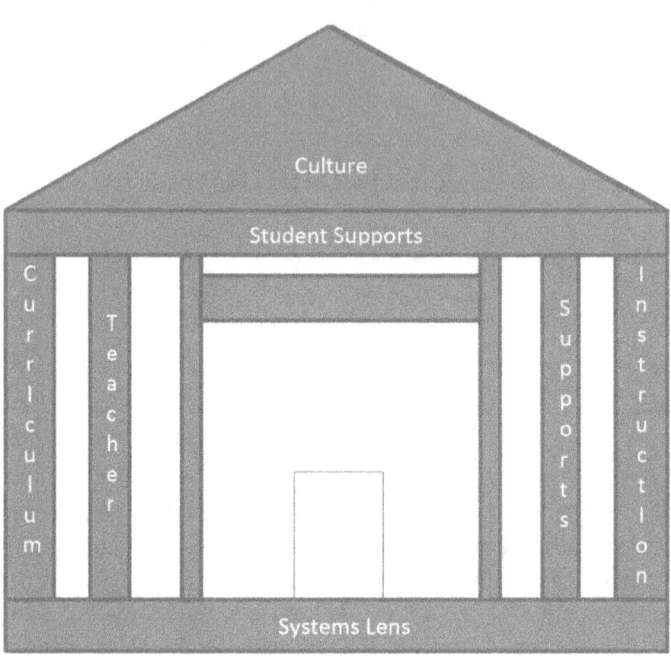

Figure C.1 Systems in School Leadership.

In *The Final Piece: A Systems Approach to School Leadership,* it is highlighted that both of the first two systems must work in concert to support and give direction to student support systems. Without student support systems, teachers are teaching, but no one can assure that all students are learning. In this book, the comprehensive student support system required is addressed. Additionally, the culture system is addressed. Remember, culture can be created and should be intentional.

In the construction field, one can often find a building project that is unfinished. Maybe the builder ran out of funds or ran into some other limiting factors. Whether the house is framed but does not have a roof or the support beams are not in place, the house is still inhabitable. What happens to that property? What happens to all of the resources expended to that point? Education is famous for expending funds that do not lead to attaining the final product desired.

As represented in the two books, all four systems must work in concert. School systems should be designed for success, which means they need to be complete and work in concert with one another. Developing the right systems will allow you to do your job more effectively and will allow teachers and students to experience success. All of these systems impact your culture as well. Don't let your resources decay before your eyes.

About the Author

Dr. Lee Westberry comes to education via an unusual route. Her first degree was in business administration. After working in business and industry, Dr. Westberry was committed to addressing the deficiencies with communication and computational skills she found in the workforce. Therefore, she decided to go back to school to teach. She flipped a coin to determine if she would teach English or mathematics, and English won the coin toss.

Dr. Lee Westberry has over twenty years of experience as a school administrator. She has served as a middle-school principal, a high-school principal, and a district supervisor in more than one capacity. Before serving as an administrator, Dr. Westberry was an English teacher in more than one school system.

Most recently, Dr. Westberry serves as the educational leadership program coordinator and assistant professor of educational leadership in the Zucker Family School of Education at The Citadel in Charleston, South Carolina. In addition to teaching classes in the master's program and educational specialist program, Dr. Westberry also supports principal leaders in the form of principal service. In this capacity, Dr. Westberry travels across the state to provide professional learning experiences for sitting principals.

Dr. Westberry is also the CEO of the F.L.I.P. Educational Group, LLC (Focused Leadership in Practice), which serves to consult with districts and schools, providing training for teaching staffs, instructional coaches, and principals where needed.

In addition to her passion for education, Dr. Westberry has a passion for her family. Married for over twenty-eight years to her high-school sweetheart, she strives to be the best wife to Danny and mother to her two smart and beautiful daughters, Warner and Sophie.

The Final Piece: A Systems Approach to School Leadership is the sequel to *Putting the Pieces Together: A Systems Approach to School Leadership*. Dr. Westberry plans to continue sharing her experience and practical solutions through more *Putting the Pieces Together* texts.

www.ingramcontent.com/pod-product-compliance
Lightning Source LLC
Chambersburg PA
CBHW071832230426
43672CB00013B/2826